25 Projects
for Horsemen

25 Projects
for Horsemen

Money-Saving,
Do-It-Yourself Ideas for the
Farm, Arena, and Stable

Jessie Shiers
and
Jason Shiers

The Lyons Press
Guilford, Connecticut
An imprint of The Globe Pequot Press

The Lyons Press is an imprint of The Globe Pequot Press

Library of Congress Cataloging-in-Publication Data

Shiers, Jessie.
 25 projects for horsemen : money-saving, do-it-yourself ideas for the farm, arena, and stable / Jessie C. Shiers and Jason W. Shiers.
     p. cm.
 Includes index.
 ISBN 978-1-59921-212-8
 1. Horses--Equipment and supplies. 2. Stables--Management. 3. Woodwork. 4. Handicraft.
I. Shiers, Jason W. II. Title. III. Title: Twenty five projects for horsemen.
 SF285.4S55 2008
 636.1'083--dc22

                               2008024497

Printed in the United States of America

10 9 8 7 6 5 4 3 2 1

To Isabel, who was with us every step of the way.

And to Bobbie, who is in our thoughts always.

Contents

Acknowledgments

Many individuals helped in the development of the projects in this book. First and foremost we would like to thank Bill Moriarty, our neighbor and Jason's accomplice in project building. Bill showed up at our door most Saturdays and Sundays at 6:30 A.M., ready to get started. You'll see him in a few of the photos in this book. Thanks also to neighbors Lawrence White (for the tractor) and Linda Frechette (for being there).

Norm Justice provided inspiration, original stall doors, hardware, and numerous tack hooks, brackets, and saddle racks. Tody Justice consulted on the sewing projects and provided valuable insight. Dodie Kaloust helped sew the projects and provided support and good cheer. Roberta Kaloust donated materials and sewing machines. Gregg Kaloust provided great help during photo shoots and proved himself to be an able horse wrangler and heavy-stuff carrier. The Shiers and Monkiewicz families provided much of the wood used in the projects.

Thanks to Tom Moates both for his endless, infectious enthusiasm and his generous contribution of the pole shed chapter. (Be sure to look for Tom's books, *Discovering Natural Horsemanship* and the forthcoming *The Quest for Collection,* both from The Lyons Press.)

Thanks, of course, to our intrepid editor and personal friend, Steve Price, as well as to all the hands that stirred the pot at Lyons, including editors Ellen Urban, Cynthia Hughes, and Melissa Hayes, and designer Mary Ballachino.

Introduction

This book is written for the average horseperson who has some basic skills and would like to save some money, or have the satisfaction of doing the work. It assumes a basic understanding of the tools, materials, and methods needed to complete simple projects. However, none of the projects in the book require advanced skills. If you are really starting from zero and know nothing about working with wood or sewing, we recommend that you seek out some books on basic techniques before you begin.

What this book also does, hopefully, is provide you with good templates for practical and useful projects. For us, it was a great learning experience—or, that is, many learning experiences, as our vision for a project would often change during the process, and we have presented the best design here. There are many ways to build things, and we are not suggesting that the methods offered in this book are the only ways. Our projects were solutions for the specific needs of our farm: storage, horse care, organization, thriftiness, riding, jumping, and shelter (not to mention the need to use power tools to justify their purchase). We are confident that you have many of these same needs and we are honored to be able to share our ideas with you. Ultimately, you may have different requirements for your farm; we hope our projects will serve as inspiration and help you learn the necessary techniques so you can develop your own skills and solutions.

Almost all of the projects in this book will save you money. It is great if you can use salvaged or scrap material to construct some of the projects. We built many of these projects virtually for free using materials salvaged from deck-building and house construction sites of relatives and friends. But even if you must buy all brand-new materials, you still stand to save some bucks. For example, we built our lean-to shed using brand-new materials for approximately $1,000. The same shed built from a kit or by a contractor would have cost at least $4,000.

We bought all the materials needed to complete every project in the horse clothing chapter for under $120. Had we bought each item at retail, the total would have been at least twice as much. (Using average prices online: cooler, $65; memory-foam saddle pad, $75; polo wraps, $20; quarter sheet, $60; saddle cover, $20 = $240.) Even better, you can customize your horse clothing by choosing any fabric pattern available; you're not limited to the few choices offered by most retailers.

You can create an entire matching wardrobe for your horse. (Then use the same fleece to sew a vest or jacket for yourself to complete the ensemble!)

Difficulty Ratings

Each project includes a "Difficulty Rating" to help you determine in advance whether you feel up to the task. The Difficulty Rating is not a scientific measurement; it's simply an overall assessment of the amount of time, skills, tools, precision, and complexity involved in each project.

∩ *Extremely easy* and takes less than an hour to complete, requiring no specialized tools or skills. Good projects for children with supervision. (See Projects for a Rainy Day chapter.)

∩ ∩ *Easy* and can be done in a couple of hours. May require some basic sewing or wood-crafting skills, but these can be learned "on the job."

∩ ∩ ∩ *Medium-difficulty* projects that require slightly more specialized tools and skills, and will take several hours to complete.

∩ ∩ ∩ ∩ *Difficult* projects. We recommend that you practice your skills on some of the level 2 and 3 projects before tackling these harder ones if you don't have any prior experience.

∩ ∩ ∩ ∩ ∩ *Extremely difficult* and *time-consuming* projects, such as the lean-to shed. Be prepared to spend a weekend or two working on these. You may have to rent or buy some specialized equipment.

CHAPTER 1

Safety

Working with power tools is always potentially dangerous. Use common sense and safe practices when working on the projects in this book. You can minimize safety risks by taking the following precautions:

SAFETY REMINDERS

- Wear eye protection to shield your eyes from flying fragments of wood. While eye protection often makes one feel silly, it will save you from getting small pieces of sawdust thrown from a circular saw in your eye.
- When sanding with a power sander, wear a dust mask to minimize the inhalation of fine particles. It's surprising how much sanding dust can affect your breathing later that day or when you've gone to bed.
- Work carefully, always being conscious of where your fingers are in relation to any cutting blade. When working a small piece of wood on a machine such as a table saw or router, use push sticks, rather than your hands, to move the workpiece across the cutting blade.
- Clamp workpieces down securely before beginning to cut them.
- Keep tools sharp. A dull blade is a dangerous blade.
- Read all safety and instruction manuals that come with your power tools.
- Use GFCI (ground fault circuit interrupter) outlets that will shut off power in the event of an overload, short, or electrocution. Test your GFCI outlets regularly.
- Maintain a tidy, well-lit work area to avoid tripping hazards.
- Work carefully and attentively. Never rush.
- Have a partner help you to lift heavy material, such as 4x8 sheets of plywood, roofing, long lumber, and posts.
- Stop and take breaks, eat a snack, and stay hydrated. There's nothing worse than getting frustrated or overtired—you could easily make mistakes that cause you to ruin a project, waste materials, or worse, get hurt!

CHAPTER 2

Tools, Hardware, and Materials

As the saying goes, "Use the right tool for the job." In many cases, the easiest, fastest way to complete a task is to use specialized power tools such as a compound miter saw, a compressor and nailers, an impact driver, a drill, a table saw, a radial arm saw, or a router. However, the average horse owner may not have all of these tools at the ready in the garage or barn. Throughout the book we will provide options for the easier method—using a power tool made for the job—or a slightly more difficult or time-consuming method using common power tools or hand tools.

Often, the larger power tools can be rented from a local hardware store, and for large construction projects, tool rental is well worth the cost. For example, when we were pouring the footings for our shed, we rented a cement mixer for $28 per day. It saved us significant time and energy by doing the job efficiently. And don't overlook renting even small, handheld power tools for a few hours or a day, as large home improvement chains have rental departments where these tools are available at very reasonable prices. In the sections below, we describe each item and provide approximate price ranges for purchase. Rental costs for the power tools will vary according to geographic location.

HAND TOOLS

Hammer

Everyone needs a hammer or three! Hammers can be used for pounding nails, forcing a tight-fitting board into place, or pulling out nails. For the projects in this book, any hammer will do, as long as it is comfortable and well balanced in your hands. The most common hammer is the nailing claw hammer. Generally speaking, lighter hammers are suited for finishing nails or brads and lighter tasks, while a heavier hammer, called a framing hammer, is suited for more demanding tasks, such as pounding 3$\frac{1}{2}$-inch nails. Purchase price: $6 to $20.

Rubber or Wooden Mallets

There are also times when wooden or rubber mallets are needed, as when tapping parts of a project into place. A metal hammer would unnecessarily damage the wood. Purchase price: $12 to $14.

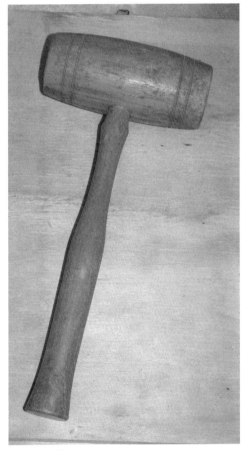

Wooden mallet.

Screwdriver

Most screws used in wood construction projects are Phillips-head screws. You will need an assortment of Phillips-head screwdrivers in various sizes. Better yet, invest in a good screw gun with a variety of bits (see below under Power Tools). Purchase price: basic set, $16; multi-head set, $30.

Handsaw

A handsaw can be used in place of a circular saw, miter saw, and table saw. For many tasks, the handsaw will be much more time-consuming and labor-intensive than the appropriate power tool, so it is usually best to opt for the power circular saw. However, in some cases, such as sawing a very short cut or a complex miter cut, nothing beats a handsaw. Also, some projects will require you to finish a cut made by a powered saw using a handsaw. So, have available a short-back handsaw with eight points per inch. Purchase price: $11 to $20.

Miter Box

A miter box is a prefabricated plastic or metal form used to help you make miter (angled) cuts with a handsaw. You place a board into the miter box, select the appropriate premeasured and labeled angle guide, and slide the handsaw through the guide to cut an accurate angle. A miter box and handsaw are an extremely affordable and functional alternative to a compound miter saw, which is a rather expensive power tool. Purchase price: $10 to $40.

Old metal miter box and handsaw assembly. Plastic versions are much less expensive and easier to find.

Socket/Ratchet Wrench and Sockets

A socket/ratchet wrench is used to tighten bolts, nuts, and lag screws. Various socket sizes are available to fit a variety of nuts, bolts, and screw heads. Metric and standard sockets are not interchangeable, so make sure your tool matches your bolt or nut. They work well for small jobs, but if you are going to be tightening a lot of bolts or lag screws through lumber or cement, an impact driver is your friend (see below under Power Tools). At the very least, we recommend having an adjustable crescent wrench on hand. Purchase price: small socket set, $20; socket set with 160 pieces or more, $80 to $100; adjustable crescent wrench set, $16.

Chisel.

Chisels

When working with wood, there are times you need to touch up an area or remove material, and there's no other way to do it but the old-fashioned way. This is when you need a chisel to go along with your hammer or mallet. Purchase price: set, approximately $30.

Locking Pliers

Locking pliers are excellent to have on hand in case you strip a screw head and need to retract the screw manually. Adjust the pliers so that they clamp tightly on the head of the screw, and then use the pliers to turn the screw to the left until it is freed. Purchase price: $13.

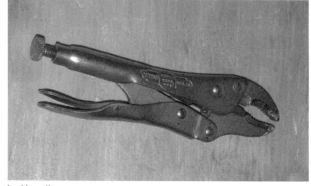

Locking pliers.

Clamps

Bar clamps: Good bar clamps are very expensive. The longer the bar clamp, the more expensive it will be. Inexpensive bar clamps have a tendency to easily bow or crown under pressure, which is why they are cheap. Clamps are quintessential tools, especially when you're working alone, so don't skimp in this department. Find a set of good-quality bar clamps that are 24 inches long, and you won't be sorry. Purchase price: $10 to $30.

Pipe clamps: Pipe clamps don't usually come with the pipes. You buy the clamping attachments, and then buy a black iron pipe of any length in the appropriate diameter to fit the clamps. Clamps come in $1/2$-inch,

Left to right: Corner clamps, C-clamps, a pipe-clamp assembly, and two sizes of bar clamps.

$3/4$-inch, and 1-inch diameters. Pipes in various lengths can be purchased relatively inexpensively in the plumbing department. Note that one end of the pipe needs to be threaded. Have on hand 2-foot, 4-foot, and 6-foot pipes, along with two sets of clamp attachments, and you can interchange the pipes into the clamps as needed. Purchase price: pair of clamps, $12; pipe, $2 per foot.

C-clamps: These are helpful when you need to secure material, such as 2x4s or plywood, to your work surface for cutting or sanding. Purchase price: $2 to $8, depending on size.

Corner clamps: These are used for making picture frames. They hold the corner miter joints together tightly while the wood glue dries. You can try to make a frame without them, but you'll get frustrated and it won't be any fun. Purchase price: $9.

Vise clamp: A clamp that is permanently attached to a workbench, used to hold workpieces tightly.

MEASURING, LEVELING, AND MARKING TOOLS

Tape Measure

Of course, you need a measuring tape. You can complete any of the projects in this book with a standard 25-foot tape. We find it's best to have several on hand, since they always seem to be missing when you need them. However, note that no two tapes measure exactly the same, due to subtle differences in manufacturing. So, do your best to stick with the same tape for a project that requires precise or intricate measurements. Purchase price: $8 to $20.

Rulers

While tape measures are good for measuring for initial cuts, finer measurements are needed when laying out project pieces for assembly or when measuring spaces that a tape measure cannot fit or bend into. This is when it is necessary to use a 6-inch ruler with edges graduated in 8ths and 16ths, or in 32nds and 64ths. A steel ruler with finely etched black lines is good for easy reading and longevity. Plastic or wooden rulers bend, chip, and break easily. Purchase price: $25 for a high-quality steel ruler.

Levels

Carpenter's level: When joining wood or building structures, all the elements need to be level (straight across) and plumb (straight up and down). A carpenter's level has three separate vials with bubbles that enable you to check if boards or posts are level and plumb. When the level is level or plumb, the appropriate bubble will be centered between two marks. Purchase price: $26 and up for a 48-inch aluminum level.

Line level: This is a very simple device that hangs on a horizontal string, usually used when constructing the initial site plan for a large structure, such as a lean-to. Purchase price: $2.

Torpedo level: A torpedo level is essentially a 6- or 9-inch-long version of a carpenter's level. Purchase price: $3 and up.

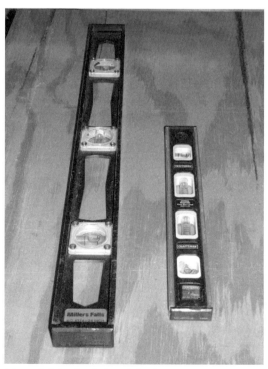

A carpenter's level and a torpedo level.

Laser level: If you plan to build a large structure like a lean-to, we recommend buying or renting a laser level, for precision when determining height measurements. Chain home improvement stores offer inexpensive laser levels. A laser level will enable you to determine the exact height measurement for posts and rooflines, to compensate for any slope that may exist, and to ensure that the structure you build will be level.

We call them bobble heads, since they sit on a tripod and can be maneuvered. You adjust the "head" until it is level, and then it shoots a laser that shows the level line on a surface. You can move the laser line to the right or left, and it will stay level. Purchase price: $30 to $400 and up (not including tripod), depending on features and quality.

Squares

Another important measuring device is the square. We use two types of squares in this book— a framing square and a speed square. A framing square has a long, 2-inch-wide rule and a short $1^{1}/_{2}$-inch rule, which meet at a 90-degree angle. The wider rule is known as the *blade;* the narrower one is the *tongue.* The

Framing square.

square has many uses, including laying out rafters and squaring boards at butt joints. The speed square is a triangular measuring tool that can be used to measure, find angles, or to simply enable you to mark perpendicular lines. Purchase price: framing square, $6; speed square, $7 to $12.

Chalk Line

A chalk line is invaluable when measuring, marking, and cutting long straight lines. The chalk line consists of a long strand of heavy string rolled up inside a dispenser filled with blue chalk. Measure and mark two points, pull out the string and stretch it tight between the marks, and then lift the string between two fingers, letting it snap back down

Chalk line.

onto the workpiece. This will leave a clear, straight line for you to cut. The chalk is easy to dust off afterward. Purchase price: $8 to $10.

POWER TOOLS

Screw Gun

If you plan to build any of the wooden projects in this book, we strongly recommend the purchase of a decent screw gun (power screwdriver). The time it will save over a hand screwdriver is enormous. You will soon find yourself using your screw gun for every little task, from mounting bucket holders to fixing the fence line. You'll wonder how you ever survived without one! They are available in either cordless (battery-powered) or plug-in models. Cordless models may be slightly more expensive, but they are worth it for the flexibility and ease of use. Prices vary greatly, but keep in mind that you get what you pay for in terms of quality, especially for cordless models. The battery provides the power, and a good battery is very expensive. Corded models will give you more power for your dollar, but you will be tied to the wall outlet. Purchase price: $80 and up for a cordless model.

Drill

To prevent splitting your wood, you will need to use a drill to predrill pilot holes for screws. A combination screw gun/drill has a switch that changes it from screwing to drilling functions. We use our screw gun/drill on nearly every project. However, to save time spent switching back and forth between a drill bit and a screwdriver bit, it is ideal to have two separate tools, one dedicated to each task. There are times when you will need

Cordless and plug-in models. Both of these tools can be used as either a drill or a screw gun.

a corded drill, such as drilling into concrete, since it can draw as much power as it needs to get the job done. Cordless models may not have enough power for the toughest jobs. We recommend having both a cordless screw gun/drill combination, and a corded power drill. Purchase price: $25 to $200 and up.

Drill Bits

Multipurpose bits, as well as tapered drill and countersinking bits, are needed for most of the woodworking projects. Tapered drill and countersinking drill bits are used to predrill pilot holes; the countersink part of the bit, which usually has a stop collar to prevent over-drilling, creates a conical recess at the top of the hole into which the screw head can sit so it is flush with, or below, the surface of the wood. Predrilling pilot holes prevents unnecessary damage to the wood, such as splitting. If you don't

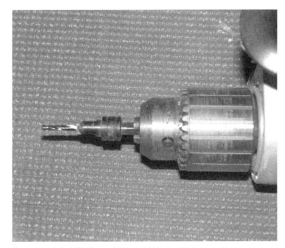

A countersink drill bit, used to predrill holes for screws leaving a shallow recess for the head of the screw to sink into.

predrill and countersink, you are bound to ruin your projects when the wood inevitably splits. You can purchase multipurpose bits in a set with varying diameters and depths. You'll probably have to purchase countersinking bits separately, but simple sets can be found at specialty woodworking stores like Rockler. Purchase price: 16-piece bit set, $25; countersinking bit, $5 to $10 each.

Table Saw

A table saw consists of a circular, spinning saw blade mounted to a motor under a tabletop. The blade protrudes through the surface and can be adjusted to different heights, and sometimes angles, depending upon the model. It is used to make long, straight cuts by sliding the workpiece across the tabletop and through the saw blade. The workpiece is guided through by a fence, which is an adjustable bar that slides back and forth across the table to set the desired width of the cut. A table saw is a very versatile power tool, and is often the first large purchase for the hobbyist or woodworker. However, it is not 100

Contractor table saw.

percent necessary that you purchase one. We were able to construct all the projects in this book without a table saw. We often used a handheld circular saw or router instead.

There are two types of table saws that you might want to consider: benchtop and contractor. Benchtop saws are mounted to the top of a workbench, and usually have smaller, direct-drive motors. Contractor table saws are heavier and larger, and are attached to a metal stand or base. Many have belt-driven motors. A contractor saw enables you to work with larger material, such as plywood. It's harder to make long, straight cuts on a benchtop table saw. A typical table saw has a 10-inch blade. Purchase price: $150 and up.

Circular Saw

Circular saw.

A circular saw is the same thing as a table saw, but without the table. It is a handheld tool that can be used to make straight or angled cuts. A separate guide or fence can be clamped to the workpiece to ensure a straight cut. A typical circular saw has a $7^1/_4$-inch blade. Purchase price: $40 and up.

Router

A router is a specialized tool used primarily to bevel the edges of a piece of wood, providing a finished look. A variety of bits are available in styles ranging from sim-

A router mounted to a handmade router table.

ple to elaborate. The most commonly used bit is a round-over bit, which simply creates a rounded edge. The router can be held in the hand, or it can be mounted under a router table. Although the tool looks relatively benign, the sharp spinning blade makes the router one of the more dangerous tools in the workshop. Be careful not to let your fingers get too close to the bit while beveling a workpiece. Also be aware that the bit can catch and throw small fragments, or even the entire workpiece, so always wear eye protection and use caution when working with a router. Purchase price: router, $90 and up; router table, $40 and up.

Compound Miter Saw

A compound miter saw is a large, expensive, highly specialized power tool used to make precise angled cuts in wood. It is a time-saver for sure, but not necessarily worth the purchase price for the average horse owner. If you have a miter saw, by all means use it. You will see it mentioned in the Tools list in many of the woodworking projects. If you do not have a miter saw, never fear. You can achieve the same results by expending more time and effort using a miter box and handsaw (see above under Hand Tools). Miter saws are also available for rent at many hardware stores. Purchase price: $100 and up.

Compound miter saw.

Jigsaw

A jigsaw is a handheld device with a narrow, straight, serrated, reciprocating blade that enables you to make curved cuts in a board. It is often used for projects that require complex cuts. Purchase price: $50 and up.

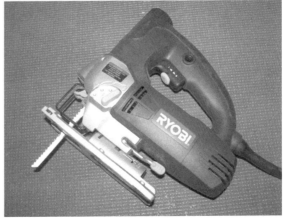

Jigsaw.

Random-Orbit Sander

Handheld power sanders come in several types, and we recommend the random-orbit style. A power sander is a relatively inexpensive purchase and can save a lot of time, so if you plan to build multiple wood projects, it might be a good investment. In addition, if you have a good eye and a steady hand, a power sander can perform some of the tasks of a router, such

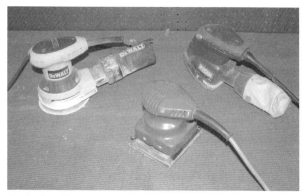

A selection of power sanders.

as beveling the edge of a board. Purchase price: $35 and up.

Air Compressor and Nail Guns

Another pricey time-saver, a pneumatic nailer is a great tool for both construction and finish work—if you happen to have one. You will need at least two guns—one for heavy construction nails and one for smaller finish nails or brads—which both attach to the same air compressor. Lacking an air compressor, you can simply use the old standby—a hammer. Tasks will take much longer and you will get a good bicep workout, but the cost, of course, is far less. Air compressors and guns are well worth the price of rental for larger construction projects such as the lean-to shed. Purchase price: portable set including three guns, $250 to $300.

Portable air compressor.

Impact Driver or Impact Wrench

An impact driver (wrench) enables you to simultaneously screw and

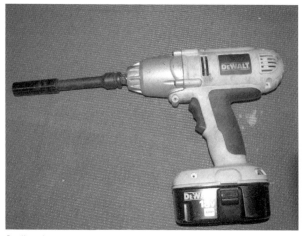

Cordless impact driver, or hammer drill.

pound large fasteners, such as lag screws or bolts, into wood or cement—for example, when attaching a ledger board to the side of a building using 6-inch lag screws. While one could ratchet the screws by hand, this would require enormous energy and lots of time. Note that an impact wrench requires impact sockets, as it will destroy regular sockets. Purchase price: corded, $130 and up; cordless, $200 and up.

Reciprocating Saw

A reciprocating saw is a handheld tool with a large, heavy-duty serrated blade that can be used to remove objects or materials that are in your way. If you don't care how something looks, just cut it off with a reciprocating saw. It's a "git 'er done" tool. It cuts quickly, and if you have a demolition blade, it will cut through anything, including steel bars. In the lean-to project, for example, we needed to remove preexisting material from the sides and roof of our barn before putting up the new ledger board, rafters, and roof. Purchase price: $50 and up.

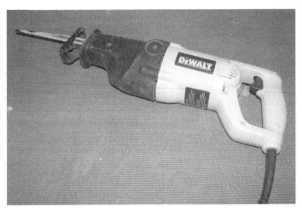
Reciprocating saw.

FASTENERS

Screws

While there are many types of screws, we typically used countersunk screws for our projects. The head of a countersunk screw is conical, with a flat outer face and tapering inner face, allowing it to sink below the surface of the wood. Standard-size screws we used were #6, #8, and #10, with lengths ranging between $3/4$-inch and 3 inches. The numbers refer to the diameter of the head, so the #6 screw is smaller and narrower than the #10 screw. The screws for our projects required #1 and #2 Phillips-head drive bits.

Lag Screws and Washers

A lag screw usually has a square or hexagonal head that requires a wrench or socket driver rather than a screwdriver. These are large, structural fasteners used in framing, building construction, and any time large lumber needs to be fastened in a permanent way. We used them in constructing jump standards, for example, since there is no chance that they will work free over time, like screws or nails can, and they can be easily retightened if the wood shrinks. A metal washer should be inserted along with a lag screw to prevent the head of the screw from sinking into the hole made by the screw itself. (See the sidebar on page 75.)

Nails

We primarily used nails driven by air-compressor-powered nail guns (see under Power Tools, above). Use finish nails (16-gauge) and brad nails (18-gauge), which are very narrow, on finer projects such as the tack trunk or grooming box, or any project where appearance matters. Such nails have very small heads so that they can be driven deeply into the wood and the surface holes can be hidden with wood filler.

We used larger nails in the lean-to project, as well as the jumps. We often used a few nails to quickly join boards together to hold them in place while we followed up with screws or lag screws. Common nail lengths are between 8d and 16d (the "d" is pronounced "penny"), which are between $2\frac{1}{2}$ and $3\frac{1}{2}$ inches long.

MATERIALS: WOOD

A Note about Measurements

Dimension lumber (known in contractor terms as "S4S") is wood that has been cut and planed smooth on all four sides and is ready to be used. This is the type of wood you will find at most home supply stores. An important thing to realize when working with S4S lumber is that the nominal size is actually not the true size of the wood. For example, a standard 2x4 is *not* 2 inches by 4 inches. Measure one and see for yourself. It is actually $1\frac{1}{2}$ inches thick by $3\frac{1}{2}$ inches wide. This is because the original rough-cut 2x4 has been dried and planed on all sides, reducing the overall width and depth. The reference chart below provides an overview of the sizes used for the projects in this book. (Note: The length of a board is usually given in feet and reflects the true length of the board—so, for example, a 2x4x8 board is $1\frac{1}{2}$ inches thick by $3\frac{1}{2}$ inches wide by 8 feet long.)

Dimensions of Standard Lumber

NAME	TRUE SIZE
⁵⁄₄ (1¼ inches)	1 inch thick
1x3	¾ x 2½
1x4	¾ x 3½
2x4	1½ x 3½
2x6	1½ x 5½
2x8	1½ x 7¼
2x10	1½ x 9¼

Also, we sometimes refer to "⁵/₄ board," which is pronounced "five-quarter." This lumber is measured in ¹/₄-inch increments, so its nominal thickness is 1¹/₄ inch. The true measurement is actually 1 inch thick. So, for example, ⁵/₄x6 S4S lumber is actually 1 inch x 5¹/₂ inches.

Rough-cut lumber is also available at a lower cost, which you may choose to use for larger construction projects such as stalls, stall doors, run-in sheds, and barn doors. The stated size is usually an accurate measurement of the true dimensions of the board. It is a good idea to measure rough lumber before using it to determine its exact measurements, since there is some variability. While it costs less to buy, rough-cut lumber does not have a finished appearance; thus, the term *rough*. It can give you splinters easily, and it takes a lot of sanding to produce a smooth and stainable surface. However, don't let this deter you from using rough lumber; it is used throughout many of our projects in this book! Even if you don't sand or finish it at all, its rustic appearance is sometimes desirable.

Pine

In most geographic locations, pine is the least expensive wood to buy and the most readily available. The standard 2x4 is made of pine, and it is readily available in a variety of other dimensions. Pine has many benefits, including its low cost, light weight, and ease of use. Because it is so soft, it is easy to cut and drill. It is less likely to split when you drive a nail or screw into it. Staining pine is a lot of fun, as a finished project made of pine is quite beautiful. For first-time woodworkers, pine is the ideal material.

Poplar

Poplar is an excellent choice for projects that will be painted rather than stained. It is extremely smooth and flat when sanded, and takes paint very well. The native color of the wood can be inconsistent, sometimes tending toward greenish, but a couple coats of paint do the trick. Poplar is technically a hardwood, but is still soft enough to allow easy woodworking.

Oak

Oak is the ultimate in durability, beauty, and class for indoor finished projects such as picture frames, cabinets, and furniture. It is more expensive and also much harder than pine and poplar. Due to its hardness, it is much more difficult for the novice woodworker to craft. It requires careful predrilling, as it splits easily when nails or screws are driven into it. It is also very heavy, so it is not the best choice for larger portable projects such as a tack trunk or saddle stand.

Hemlock

We use rough-cut hemlock for most of our large construction projects, such as stalls, stable and barn doors, and sheds. A relatively inexpensive wood, it weathers well and provides a rustic appearance. The wood is easy to cut, nail, and screw into.

Cedar

A very lightweight and soft wood, cedar has a natural resistance to insects and rot, so it virtually does not decay. Well known for its aromatic properties, cedar is a nice choice for storage projects such as the tack trunk, saddle stand, or saddle cabinet. Its distinctive rosy colors and vibrant character make cedar a beautiful wood to use for clear-finished decorative indoor projects. However, it is quite expensive.

Pressure-Treated

Pressure-treated wood is ideal for exterior applications in locations where the seasons are wet, rainy, and snowy. The wood has undergone a chemical process that makes it a durable outdoor building product that's resistant to insects and rot. Before 2003, arsenic was used in the treatment process, which made it dangerous to use around animals, such as horses, that would chew on it. Today's pressure-treated lumber is safe for animals, pets, and children. While it is rugged, it is also very expensive and really heavy. We used it mainly in the jumps chapter, as these projects remain outside year-round and they're in direct contact with the ground.

Plywood

Plywood is a convenient product to use for large projects such as cabinets and trunks. Made of multiple sheets of very thin wood bonded together with adhesive, good-quality plywood is actually stronger than comparably sized solid wood boards. It is sold in a large variety of thicknesses, qualities, and prices, all in a standard size of 4 feet by 8 feet (true dimensions). Choose plywood based on your needs, in terms of thickness and grades. There are three common grades to consider: AA, AC, and CDX. There are other common grades—such as oriented strand board (OSB) and particle board—but we did not use these types of plywood in our projects.

AA plywood is top quality. It is smooth and clear of knotholes, front and back. While we did not use it, AA would be ideal for the tack trunk and saddle cabinet. It depends on whether appearance is important on both the inside and outside of such projects. One can also purchase AA plywood that is made from hardwood, such as poplar, oak, and maple.

For our needs, we chose the mid-grade AC plywood for the tack trunk and the saddle cabinet, as one side of the wood is clear of knots.

In projects that require rugged stuff, CDX is appropriate. CDX plywood is inexpensive, although sometimes a bit unattractive.

Each grade of plywood can be purchased in different thicknesses. Half-inch or thinner plywood tends to warp and bow when used across very large expanses, so choose $3/4$-inch plywood for these applications. Last, please note that the nominal thickness of plywood is not its true dimension. For $1/2$-inch and $3/4$-inch plywood, the actual thicknesses are $15/32$ and $23/32$ respectively, which is $1/32$ inch less than the nominal size. In our projects, we did not bother to factor in this slight difference, as it did not affect the finished work.

Exotic Species

Exotic species of wood are unique-looking and very expensive types such as curly maple, purpleheart, ebony, mahogany, rosewood, and figured walnut. You may choose to use these woods for small pieces of larger projects (such as the bridle bracket on the saddle stand) or small-scale projects such as picture frames or whip holders. It's always wise to practice first on a cheaper wood, such as pine, to avoid making mistakes with the expensive wood. Check the scrap bin at woodworking stores to find small pieces that are relatively inexpensive. You'll not only be able to make a beautiful craft, but you'll also be saving precious wood from the incinerator.

Places to Find Free Wood

There are many ways to acquire free or very inexpensive wood that can be used for a variety of projects. Often you just need to be in the right place at the right time. We always have our eyes open and will grab any wood we find, as long as it is in good condition. Even heavily weathered wood from an old barn can be made to look new again by re-planing or sanding it.

In all cases, be sure to ask first before scavenging! *Do not* wander into a landfill or construction site without permission. Here are some common places to look:

- Habitat for Humanity ReStores (www.habitat.org/env/restores.aspx)
- Your local transfer station or landfill
- Construction sites
- Demolition sites
- Scrap wood from your own earlier projects
- Old barns or sheds that are being torn down
- Broken furniture from yard sales or the attics of relatives

SANDING, STAINING, AND FINISHING

Sanding

For basic hand-sanding jobs, you will need to purchase a sanding block and stock up on sandpaper of three different grits: 60-grit for the initial smoothing of the wood, 100-grit for a finer surface, and 220-grit to sand between coats of finish. A sanding block is designed to hold a sheet of sandpaper between clips or clamps. Good sanding blocks are molded to fit in your hand. A cost-free block is a spare piece of wood, such as a 6-inch 2x4, with a sheet of sandpaper folded around it.

For larger jobs, or if you plan to make several wood projects, a power sander is a wise investment (see Random-Orbit Sander under Power Tools above). You'll need the same selection of sandpaper grits as with hand-sanding—60-grit, 100-grit, and 220-grit. Make sure you purchase sandpaper pads that fit your particular sander model.

Staining and Finishing

Weather is an important factor to consider. The temperature needs to be above 50 degrees Fahrenheit and the climate must be dry when staining, painting, or finishing your projects. Different stains and finishes vary in the amount of drying time needed before sanding and applying a second coat. Be sure to read the label on the can for specific instructions.

There are a number of different finishes to complete woodworking projects, such as varnish, stain, polyurethane, shellac, epoxy, and paint. Entire books have been written on finishing techniques and products, so we won't go into them in detail here. Our personal favorite finish is shellac, as it is quick to dry and allows you to apply many coats in a short amount of time. We used an amber-colored shellac for the tack trunk and saddle cabinet. The finish not only provides a protective layer, but it also enhances the overall aesthetics of the project.

SEWING TOOLS AND MATERIALS

Sewing Machine

If you have a lot of time to kill, you could theoretically sew anything by hand . . . but personally, we'd rather be riding! You can complete all of the sewing projects in the Horse Clothing chapter with any basic sewing machine. More expensive models may have extra fun features such as special decorative stitches, automated embroidery, or automatic buttonholers. These features allow you to personalize your projects with monogramming or embroidery, but they are not necessary.

Fleece

Most of the sewing projects in this book are made with synthetic fleece. It's stretchy, soft, and wicks moisture. Any fabric store or website will have a large selection of patterned or solid fleece. Always choose the thickest fleece you can find. The best choice is the Polartec brand, available through www.milldirecttextiles.com.

When shopping for fabric, be sure to visit the discount bin first. Most stores have a few bolts of discontinued patterns or styles that can be bought for just a dollar or two per yard. Doesn't hurt to look!

Embellishments

Fabric and craft stores generally have a selection of appliqué patches that give the appearance of embroidery. Look for some that suit your style and color choices, and use them to personalize your projects. While most patches are sold as "iron-on," it's usually best to sew them on as well as ironing, to be sure they will last through the rough treatment and frequent washings we may give our horse equipment.

Hook-and-Loop Closures

You will often see us refer to "hook-and-loop closures." What is that? It's the generic term for Velcro. It is available at fabric or craft stores in various widths, lengths, and colors.

Thread

When sewing through thick fabric such as fleece and Velcro, you will want to use heavy-duty thread, along with a corresponding heavy-duty needle in your sewing machine. Choose a thread that is very similar in color to the fabric to avoid visible seams.

Marking Tools

You will need a marking pencil or chalk appropriate to the type and color of fabric, so you can predraw lines before cutting them. We found that regular chalkboard chalk works just fine on synthetic fleece fabric.

A carpenter's chalk line (see above under Hand Tools) is convenient for marking long, straight cuts.

Scissors

Don't bother with low-quality scissors. You will only drive yourself crazy. Buy a nice pair of scissors made for cutting fabric, and your projects will be so much more enjoyable to create.

Rotary Cutter and Mat

A rotary cutter is a tool like a very sharp pizza cutter. It makes it easy and quick to cut long, straight lines in fabric. You can even cut through multiple layers of thick fabric at once. You will also need a special mat to protect your floor or table from the cutting blade. Both the cutters and the mats may be purchased at fabric or craft stores.

CHAPTER 3

Tack Room

The daughter who won't lift a finger in the house is the same child who cycles madly off in the pouring rain to spend all morning mucking out a stable.

—Samantha Armstrong

A well-organized, clean, and safe tack room is a blessing in any barn. Costs for outfitting a tack room vary widely. Cheap saddle racks and bridle brackets are available for just a few dollars. Elaborate wire racking systems or custom-made wooden trunks and brass accessories can run into the thousands. The projects in this chapter are more durable and beautiful than the cheap plastic versions, and yet far less expensive to construct than purchasing high-end custom products. Plus, you will have a great sense of accomplishment when you look over the gorgeous new tack room you've built!

In most cases, overall measurements are suggested and are not set in stone. For example, our saddle cabinet is 32 inches deep, 32 inches wide, and 70 inches high. However, if you have limited space and only one small saddle to store, feel free to reduce the dimensions to fit your needs. Alternatively, if you are planning to store several large Western saddles, you may want to increase the dimensions. This is one of the benefits of building your own tack room accoutrements: You can custom-build them to your own desires.

Wood used in constructing the tack room elements can be almost any type. Since the tack room will presumably be indoors and thus protected from the weather, resistance to decay is not terribly important. Pine is certainly the easiest to work with, least expensive, and most readily available. Oak is stunning and extremely durable, but is also very expensive and heavy. Cedar is beautiful and smells lovely, but can be expensive to buy and is very soft, so it is easily damaged. Poplar is a good choice for any wooden item that is going to be painted or that will come into contact with expensive leather items, since it is very smooth and splinter-free when sanded and finished properly.

You can also consider mixing different types of wood for an interesting and artistic appearance. For example, the body of our saddle stand is made of pine. The slats on which the saddle rests are poplar, to protect the saddle panels from splinters and scratches. Poplar and pine are both light-colored woods with a similar appearance. However, the bridle bracket on the end is made of dark reddish-colored Western red cedar. The contrasting color is striking and attractive.

Other opportunities for using exotic, expensive woods are the smaller projects. Since they require so little wood, the expense of purchasing pricier wood is minimized. (It's not a bad idea to practice first using pine. If you make mistakes, you won't be wasting your precious mahogany or tiger maple!) The grooming box and the whip holder are both small projects that can be made with exotic wood.

Saddle Stand

Difficulty Rating: ∩ ∩ ∩ ∩

This stylish and useful saddle stand has several functions. The rounded top mimics the shape of a horse's back to gently hold an English or Western saddle in the correct form, supporting the tree and preventing the leather from becoming dented or curled. The handy tool tray at the bottom can be used for storing leather-care items, grooming tools, or wraps. A bridle hook fastened to the end completes the one-stop tack storage unit.

Poplar is the best wood to use for the top of the stand, since it is extremely smooth and splinter-free so it won't damage the underside of your saddles. It takes stain or paint easily. For the front and back, use a 2-foot-square piece of $^3/_4$-inch AC-grade plywood, which you can easily find at a large chain hardware store. There's no need to buy a full 4x8 sheet of plywood, which would require a truck for transport and excessive cutting and waste.

You can make this project with either nails or screws. We used screws, which hold the wood together more effectively than nails. If you use screws, however, you will need to predrill pilot holes and countersink, which will prevent damage to the wood, such as splitting.

Saddle Stand

Tools

- Jigsaw
- Miter saw or circular saw
- Screw gun
- Drill with #8 tapered drill bit and countersink
- Random-orbit sander
- 60- and 220-grit sandpaper
- Air compressor with finish nailer and 2½-inch finish nails
- Tape measure
- Carpenter's square
- C-clamps or bar clamps
- (Optional) Router with a round-over bit

Materials

- One 24x24-inch square of ¾-inch-thick plywood
- Seven 2-foot 1x2s, poplar (rounded top)
- Two 36-inch-long 1x4s (legs)
- Two 36-inch-long 2x4s (feet)
- One 24-inch-by-24-inch square of ½-inch birch plywood
- Two 24-inch-long 1x4s (tool tray sides)
- One 21-inch-long 1x4 (tool tray bottom)
- One bridle bracket
- #8 1¼-inch stainless steel wood screws
- #8 2-inch stainless steel wood screws and/or 2½-inch finishing nails (18-gauge)
- Wood glue

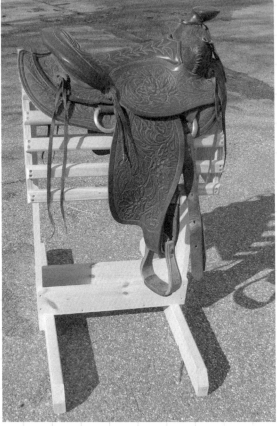

The saddle stand in action.

Building the Saddle Stand

1. Use a tape measure and mark approximately 1 inch down from the top of the end of each 36-inch 2x4 foot. Use a speed square to mark a 45-degree angle from the mark to the top of each foot. Then, cut along this line on each board to miter the corners. (Note: The length of the feet makes for a really sturdy stand. However, you might choose to use shorter feet if space is an issue.)

2. Use a router (with a round-over bit) or a sander (using 60-grit paper) to bevel the top edges of the 1x2 boards for the rounded top, the outside edges of the feet, and the outside edges of the tool tray.

3. Predrill and countersink two diagonally opposite holes on one end of each of the 36-inch 1x4 legs. Make sure the holes are no more than

3½ inches from the end, as these holes are for the screws that will attach the 2x4 feet. Next, center the legs along the outside of the feet, following the diagram. Use the speed square to ensure that the two pieces are centered

Beveling the edges of the 1x2s using a router and router table. Always keep your fingers well clear of the cutting blade.

Saddle stand (side view)

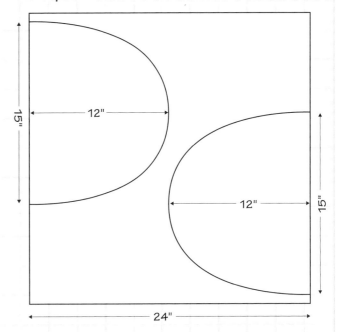

Template for ends of saddle

and squared properly. Attach using #8 2-inch screws.

4. Predrill and countersink pilot holes on each end of the 24-inch 1x4 tool tray sides and bottom. Attach the tool tray sides to the vertical legs using 2½-inch screws. Use a square to check that the legs and feet remain square and plumb.

5. Using a soft lead pencil, transfer the template on this page to the 24x24-inch plywood square. Clamp the plywood securely to a workspace or table. Using a jigsaw, cut out the rounded shape. Repeat for the second piece needed to complete the front and back.

6. The plywood pieces are attached to the outside of each leg. Make a straight line on the outside of each leg measuring 24¾ inches up from the bottom. Align the bottom (straight) edge of one of the rounded plywood pieces with the line

Use a jigsaw to cut out the pattern on the plywood.

on one leg (see diagram). Attach the plywood using #8 1¼-inch screws. Again, predrill and countersink the pilot holes to protect the wood from splitting. Repeat the process for the other plywood piece.

7. Next, attach the seven 1x2s to the plywood ends to create the rounded top. First use one of the 1x2s as a measuring device to measure and mark equal distances along the rounded edges of the plywood sides, as shown. Then have a helper hold each 1x2 piece in place while you predrill straight pilot holes and countersinks, and attach them using #8 2-inch screws.

Saddle Stand cont'd

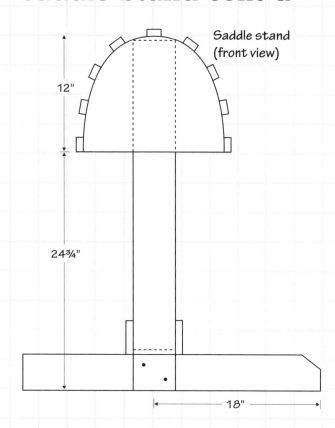

Saddle stand
(front view)

12"

24¾"

18"

Mark the locations of the 1x2s with a pencil.

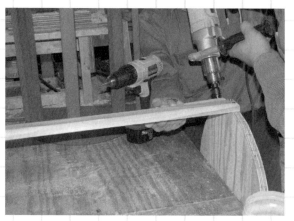

Predrill the screw holes through the 1x2s and the plywood.

8. Sand the entire project, first using the 60-grit paper, paying special attention to the top surface where the saddle will rest.

9. Finish the project with stain and polyurethane, or paint it in your stable colors. If you use a stain and polyurethane, re-sand after the first coat has dried using 220-grit sandpaper. Then apply the second coat of polyurethane.

10. Attach a bridle hook to one end of the saddle stand.

Option

Instead of using a commercially manufactured bridle bracket, you can create your own by using two scraps of wood. We used two pieces of 2x6 western red cedar to contrast with the bright tones of the pine and poplar. To make the top of the bracket that holds the crownpiece of the bridle, use a ½-inch (radius) x ⅝-inch (high) cove router bit and rout one side of the two pieces. Turn them around so the coves face each other and join to make the

groove in which the crownpiece will rest. Glue, predrill pilot holes, and screw them together using #8 1½-inch screws and attach to the saddle rack, as shown in the photo.

A simple bridle bracket made of two scraps of western red cedar, routed and joined together with screws.

Grooming Box with Natural Handle

Difficulty Rating: ∩ ∩

Everyone needs a portable way to store brushes, spray bottles, hoof picks, spurs, rags, and all the other small paraphernalia that go along with tacking up or grooming a horse. This unique grooming box will hold it all in style. The box itself is nothing special—just a functional storage solution. The handle, made of a piece of natural wood with the bark still on it, provides visual appeal—a new twist on an old standby.

The grooming box fits neatly under the saddle racks in the saddle cabinet on page 34.

Grooming Box

Tools

- Circular saw or miter saw
- Air compressor and nail gun with 2-inch finish nails
- Drill with 1¼-inch hole saw (a specialized drill bit attachment)
- Power sander
- 60- and 100-grit sandpaper

Materials

- Two 1x12x10½-inch boards (ends)
- Four 1x4x18-inch boards (sides)
- One 10⁷⁄₁₆ x 15⅜-inch piece of half-inch plywood (bottom)
- One 20-inch-long natural stick, with bark, approximately 1¼ inches in diameter

Making the Grooming Box

1. Cut the top corners off the end pieces. Following the diagram, measure and mark four points, 4 inches from each top corner along the top, and 4 inches from each top corner down the sides. Using a circular saw or miter saw, cut along the dotted lines on the diagram. Repeat for the second end piece.

2. Since the handle is a natural piece of wood, it probably won't conform to standard measurements, so you will have to fudge it a little. Measure the diameter of each end of the stick handle. Select a hole saw that is slightly smaller than the diameter of the stick. (In our case, the stick was approximately 1½ inches in diameter, so we used a 1¼-inch hole saw.) Measure 2 inches down from the center top of the end piece, as shown in the diagram. Use the hole saw to drill straight through the board. Repeat for the second end piece.

3. Clamp the stick handle into a countertop vise clamp, preferably one that has wooden clamps that won't damage the stick handle. If you only have a metal vise clamp, use scrap pieces of 1x4s or other wood on either side of the stick handle to protect it (see photo). Testing often against the hole drilled in the end piece, use a

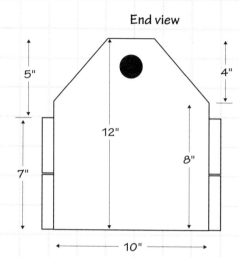

End view

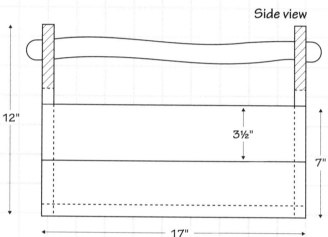

Side view

power sander or sandpaper to remove enough wood from the end of the stick so that it fits snugly into the hole. The fit should be very tight. You may need to use a rubber mallet to

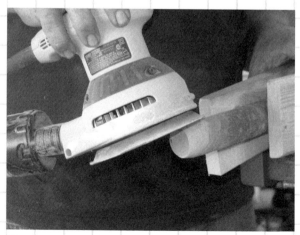

Use a power sander to reduce the diameter of the handle enough to fit into the holes on the end pieces.

pound the end piece onto the stick handle, but be careful not to be too forceful, as you could crack the end piece. Repeat for the other end of the stick handle. Check to be sure the sides are square by setting the end pieces on a table-top. Adjust by pounding with the mallet or removing more wood from the stick handle as needed.

4. Using the nail gun and 2-inch finish nails, attach the four side pieces to the end pieces as shown. Make sure that each side piece is flush with the end pieces. Be very careful to drive the nails straight, so they don't splinter out through the sides of the wood.

5. Turn the box over and insert the bottom piece. Note that the size described in the materials list is approximate. Measure the actual interior dimensions and cut the plywood exactly to fit. It should be snug, and you may have to use the rubber mallet to gently pound it into place. To secure it in place, use the nail gun and 2-inch finish nails, driven through the sides and into the bottom. Again, be very careful that the nails do not shoot out the sides of the wood. Keep your fingers clear of any area where the nail could accidentally emerge.

6. Sand the entire project, except for the natural bark handle, with a power sander, using 60-grit

Attach the sides using a nail gun.

and 100-grit sandpaper. Carefully sand the edges off of all the wood for a finished appearance.

7. Stain and finish the project as desired. We recommend applying clear polyurethane or shellac on the finished wood, which will enhance the grain and maintain the natural look.

Option

Instead of a natural handle, use a 1-inch-diameter dowel rod. Drill the holes for it with a 1-inch hole saw.

Tack Trunk

Difficulty Rating: Ω Ω Ω

Tack trunks are great for storing equipment to keep it clean and safe. They are perfect for show riders at boarding barns, since they can easily be lifted into the truck or trailer to bring all your important items along to the show, and they can be locked to prevent theft or "unauthorized borrowing."

A good-quality hardwood trunk is very valuable, and retail prices reflect that. Wooden trunks can cost as much as $1,000, and are hard to find for less than $400 (even if they are made of plywood). We built this great-looking trunk for less than $200 in materials. It is not difficult to construct, and takes only a few hours of time.

Our trunk has exterior measurements of $25\frac{1}{2}$ inches (H) x $38\frac{1}{2}$ inches (L) x $21\frac{1}{2}$ inches (D), and interior measurements of $24\frac{1}{4}$ inches (H) x 36 inches (L) x 19 inches (D). We used $\frac{1}{2}$-inch AC-grade pine plywood for the bottom, front, back, and sides, and $\frac{3}{4}$-inch AC-grade plywood for the lid top. We selected Douglas fir 1x3s for the mitered trim on the top and bottom of the main trunk box, as well as prefabricated molding to frame the front, back, and sides. We used Douglas fir 1x4s for the mitered sides that make the top lid. We finished it using amber-colored shellac to give it a rich look and a smooth, protected glossy surface.

Tack Trunk

Tools

- Circular saw or table saw
- Miter saw or handsaw and miter box
- Air compressor with finish nailer and 1- and 2-inch finish nails, crown stapler and ½-inch crown staples
- Drill and #8 predrill and countersink bit
- Screw gun and Phillips hand screwdriver
- Power sander
- 60-, 100-, and 220-grit sandpaper
- Two 4-foot pipe clamps
- Two 12-inch bar clamps

Materials

- Two 4x8 sheets of ½-inch-thick AC-grade plywood
- Three 8-foot-long Douglas fir 1x3s
- Two 6-foot-long 1x4s (same species as the 1x3s)
- One 6-foot-long strip of 1-inch corner molding
- One 36-inch piece of 2x3 (for shelf supports inside trunk)
- Three brass handles and brass fasteners
- Two brass trunk latches and brass fasteners
- One 30-inch brass piano hinge and brass fasteners
- Two brass lid supports (one left and one right)
- One brass hasp lock (if desired)
- Stain, polyurethane, shellac, or paint

Making the Tack Trunk

1. Measure and cut the plywood, 1x3s, 1x4s, and corner molding according to the diagrams, using a miter box or miter saw to cut the ends of the 1x3s and 1x4s at a 45-degree angle, as shown. For optimum use of wood and minimal waste, cut the boards as follows:
   - One 8-foot 1x3: Cut into four 21½-inch lengths with mitered ends.
   - Two 8-foot 1x3s: Cut into four 38½-inch lengths with mitered ends.
   - Two 6-foot 1x4s: Cut each 6-foot piece into one 38½-inch piece and one 21½-inch piece with mitered ends.
   - One 6-foot-long piece of 1-inch-wide molding: Cut into 17-inch strips (square cuts).
   - One 36-inch piece of 2x3: Cut into two 17-inch-long pieces.

2. You will need to make a $\frac{1}{16}$-inch-deep groove along the back top 1x3 of the main trunk box and a mirror groove on the bottom of the back 1x4 of the lid. These grooves are necessary to allow the two wings of the piano hinge to fit flush when you install it in step 11. The grooves will enable the lid to close tightly. First, start by centering the hinge evenly on the top of the 1x3 and mark the edges with a pencil. Repeat on the 1x4 for the lid. If you use a 30-inch hinge, you should have 4½ inches on either side of the hinge, measuring from the outside of the mitered corners. Now, remove

the wood to make the grooves. There are three ways to do this: A) Use a ½-inch chisel to carefully chisel out the groove. B) Use a router table, router fence, and straight bit, if you happen to have these tools. C) Use a pencil to shade a space representing the length and thickness of the hinge and then use a power sander with 60-grit paper or a hand planer to remove the wood. The sander takes the most time but gives you the most control. Simply sand evenly until the pencil shading is gone. Check the depth with the hinge and repeat the sanding process until the hinge sits flush with the surfaces of the 1x3 and 1x4.

3. Use 4-foot pipe clamps to assemble the plywood pieces into the two sides, front, and back of the trunk, following the diagram. Tack the pieces together using the air compressor gun and 1⅝-inch finish nails, being careful to shoot straight so the nails don't splinter out the sides of the wood. Keep fingers clear while using the nail gun.

4. Insert the bottom into the box. It should be a tight fit, and may need to be pounded gently into place using a mallet. Tack it in place using the finish nails along the front, sides, and back.

5. Assemble the mitered 1x3s around the bottom and top of the box following the diagram, and tack them in place using 1-inch finish nails, shooting the nails from the inside of the box

Tack Trunk cont'd

outward so as not to mar the visible surfaces of the 1x3s.

6. At each of the four outside corners of the box, use a 17-inch strip of corner molding to cover the raw edge of the plywood. Attach using the crown stapler and ½-inch crown staples.

7. Use #8 or #10 1-inch brass wood screws to reinforce all of the trim, working from the inside of the box so as not to mar the outer surfaces. You do not need to predrill if you screw from inside of the box.

8. Assemble the lid using the mitered 1x4s and ¾-inch plywood, following the diagram. We recommend gluing the 1x4s to the lid. Once you've applied a strip of glue, use the pipe clamps to attach the sides of the lid first. Align the inside of the mitered edges with the corners of the plywood lid. Attach using the nail gun and 2-inch finish nails. Repeat the process for the longer mitered 1x4s for the front and the back. Then predrill pilot holes and countersink #8 1½-inch brass wood screws evenly

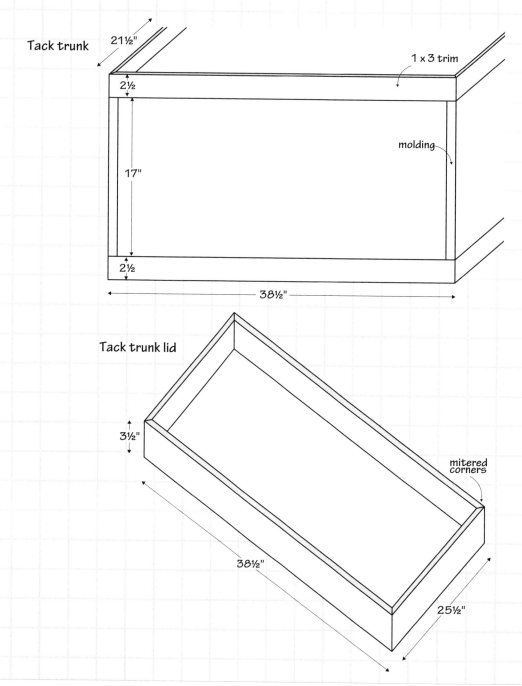

Tack trunk

21½"

1 x 3 trim

2½

17"

molding

2½

38½"

Tack trunk lid

3½"

mitered corners

38½"

25½"

along the face of the 1x4s and plywood top to reinforce the strength of the lid.

9. Using brass screws, install the 17-inch 2x3 shelf supports to hold up a standard 17-inch grooming tote. We screwed from the outside of the box in. Use 12-inch bar clamps to help keep the 2x3 supports in place. To allow the lid to close tightly, but to maximize the interior space of the trunk, attach the shelf supports approximately 4 inches below the top of the main trunk box. (You may need to adjust this depth depending upon the height of your tote's handle.)

10. Stain or paint the box and lid as desired.

Lid lifters.

We used shellac, which gave the trunk a beautiful amber glow.

11. Once the stain or paint has dried, attach the lid to the box using the piano hinge. First, use the manufacturer's fasteners to attach one wing of the piano hinge in the groove made earlier on the lid. Make sure you have the piano hinge oriented in the correct swinging direction. Next, place the lid on the box and position until the other wing is aligned correctly in the groove of the 1x3 on the main trunk box.

Attach using just one screw on each end first and close the lid to check for proper alignment. If it fits, screw in the remaining screws.

12. Install the lid supports, trunk latches, hasps, and handles following the manufacturer's instructions provided with the hardware.

Option

We wanted to protect the bottom of our tack trunk from moisture that might damage it if the wood bottom were to rest on the ground. In order to protect the cabinet, we attached four plastic feet, one in each corner on the bottom, known as nail glides. Since the plywood bottom is only ½ inch thick, we needed to provide more depth for the nail glide, so we inserted and attached 3-inch-square pieces of plywood, using a crown stapler, on the inside of the trunk box in the corners. Then, we tipped the trunk box on its side and installed the 1-inch nail glides using a wooden mallet.

Saddle Cabinet

Difficulty Rating: ∩ ∩ ∩ ∩

This large cabinet is meant to stay in one place in the tack room (as opposed to being lugged to shows and events like the tack trunk). It keeps your tack and equipment free of dust, well organized, and tidy. The cabinet also makes a handsome addition to your barn.

The cabinet has enough room for two saddle racks, and features a large lower shelf for saddle pads, grooming boxes, or boots, with space underneath for blankets or coolers. The smaller side shelf can hold bottles or other smaller items. Bridle brackets on the left hold bridles, halters, lead lines, longeing equipment, and other strap goods, while the smaller hooks on the right can carry helmets, spurs, and crops.

At 32 inches wide, 32 inches deep, and 70 inches tall, these plans will build a cabinet that is roomy enough for two Western saddles. English saddles are much smaller, so if you only ride English and space is at a premium in your tack room, you can scale down the dimensions quite a bit. For English saddles, the interior measurements of the cabinet should be a bare minimum of 22 inches wide and 24 inches deep. (However, we still like a large cabinet even for English saddles, since it allows more space for shelves and hooks.)

Saddle Cabinet

Tools

- Circular saw or table saw
- Miter saw
- Compressor, crown stapler, brad and finishing nailer
- Drill and #8 tapered predrill and counter-sink bit
- Screw gun
- Two 12-inch bar clamps
- Two 6-foot pipe clamps
- Framing square
- Chalk line
- Measuring tape

Materials

- Three 4x8 sheets of ¾-inch plywood
- One 4x8 sheet of ½-inch plywood
- Four 8-foot 1x3s or pieces of strapping
- Two 8-foot 2x4s
- Two 6-foot 2x6s
- Six cabinet hinges
- Two door handles
- Hasp and lock
- #8 1⅝-inch wood screws
- #10 ½-inch wood screws
- 1¼-inch brad nails (18-gauge)

Making the Cabinet

1. Measure and cut the back, sides, top, bottom, and the large shelf of the cabinet from ¾-inch plywood using a table saw or circular saw. The back and two sides are the same size: 32 inches wide by 70 inches long. The top and bottom of the cabinet are both 32 inches wide x 31¼ inches deep. The shelf is 32 inches wide x 28 inches deep. The shortened depth of the large shelf will allow you room to hang long items such as girths on the back sides of the doors while still being able to close the doors.

2. Measure and cut two 2x4s to 65 inches long. These will be supportive braces in the back corners to hold the back and side walls together. Cut two more 2x4s to 29½ inches. These will be braces to attach the bottom, giving it integral support.

3. Attach the two 65-inch 2x4 braces to the sides of the back piece using 1⅝-inch screws, flush with the long sides, but ¾ of an inch down from the top to leave room for the top piece to set in. Be sure to screw from the outside through the plywood into the 2x4s so the pieces are joined tightly. (Note: Once this step is complete, there will be a space of 5¼ inches at the bottom as well. This space will come into play in step 5.)

Funky 2x4s?

You might find that your 2x4 is not straight—that it has a crown, bow, or twist. To straighten the 2x4, attach one end to the plywood first with a couple of screws, and then use bar clamps and pipe clamps to manipulate the wood and hold it in place while you drive the remaining screws.

4. Use pipe clamps to hold the two plywood sides in position against the 2x4 braces and the edges of the back plywood piece. (If you're working outside and it's windy, make sure a helper holds onto the sides!) Use 1⅝-inch screws to secure the sides (see photo). Insert the top piece into the space between the sides and back so that it rests on the tops of the 2x4s, and use pipe clamps to keep it in place. Secure it with nail gun. In the corners and centers, predrill pilot holes and use 1⅝-inch screws to reinforce the top.

5. Measuring 5¼ inches from the bottom of the cabinet sides, install the two 29½-inch 2x4s to provide side support for the plywood bottom of

Circular Saw Tips

If you use a circular saw, we recommend using a chalk line to mark cutting lines, as well as bar clamps and a long straight edge as a guide to help make accurate cuts—a straight 2x4x8 clamped to the work surface does the trick well.

Saddle Cabinet cont'd

Use pipe clamps to hold the pieces together while you attach them.

Mark the upper edge of the 2x4 with a chalk line, and measure and mark screw locations every 6 inches. Since they will be visible from the outside, you want a straight line.

the cabinet. These 2x4s need to be perpendicular to the longer 2x4s used to attach the sides. They also need to be level, since the bottom will be installed on them. Once this is complete, insert the bottom piece into the space between the sides and back, push it up to the 2x4 braces, and secure it with 1⅝-inch screws.

6. Make supports for the saddle racks. The ¾-inch plywood is not thick enough to hold saddle racks securely, so extra support must be added. Turn the cabinet right side up. Inside the cabinet, measure 9¾ inches down from the top and use a framing square to draw a pencil line straight across. Cut and install a piece of 2x6 board, 25 inches long, horizontally with its top meeting the line. Have someone hold the

Hold the braces in place with clamps, and attach them by screwing through from the outside.

2x6 level while you screw through the back of the plywood and into the 2x6 board with 1⅝-inch screws. Add another 25-inch-long 2x6 board directly below the first. These will support one saddle rack. Measure 4¾ inches down from the bottom of the lower 2x6 board and install two more 2x6 boards for the second saddle rack.

7. Center one saddle rack on the lower set of 2x6 boards and screw it in place using 1⅝-inch screws. (The center is 12½ inches from each side.) Repeat for the upper saddle rack.

8. Make the large shelf at the bottom of the cabinet. First attach a 25-inch-long 2x4 horizontally to the back of the cabinet such that its top surface is 16 inches above the bottom of the cabinet. Use a level to ensure that the 2x4 is straight. The back of the shelf will rest on this board. Next, the back corners of the large shelf need to be notched so that the back of the shelf can fit flush against the back of the cabinet. Since the vertical braces are 2x4s, the cuts

We used two pieces of plywood each to make the top and bottom, using scraps left over from the back and sides, so that we wouldn't have to cut into a fourth piece of plywood. If you choose to do this as well, brace the joints with a scrap of 1x3 as shown in the photo below.

Use a scrap of wood to reinforce the joint between the two pieces that make up the bottom of the cabinet.

in the corners of the shelf must be 3½ inches x 1½ inches to fit around them. Use a speed square to measure and mark the cuts, and use a handsaw to notch them out (see photo). The shelf also needs brackets to support it in the front. You can make simple brackets using extra plywood by simply making two identical right triangles. (We used a jigsaw to cut a dec-

Use a handsaw to cut out two corners from the shelf, so that it can fit neatly around the vertical 2x4s in the corners.

orative pattern in our shelf brackets.) Alternatively, hardware stores also offer prefabricated decorative pine shelf brackets or metal brackets. Predrill pilot holes and attach the brackets, one on either side, 16 inches up from the bottom of the cabinet and 4 inches in from the front. Once the support brackets are attached, install the shelf.

9. Make the doors and door trim. Using ½-inch AC-grade plywood, cut two pieces, each 65 inches long by 16⅞ inches wide. For each door, cut two pieces of 1x3 at 16⅞ inches long, and two at 65 inches long, with corners miter-cut at 45-degree angles, as shown in the photo. Assemble the 1x3s on the plywood door like a frame, starting with one corner first. Secure the two boards with clamps and then attach using #8 1¼-inch screws or brad nails. Repeat for the second door. Next, measure and cut two middle 1x3s 11⅞ inches long. Mark a line using a framing square at 31 inches measuring up from the bottom of each door. To create a four-panel effect, align a middle 1x3 on each door above the line and attach with screws (see photo).

The doors, exterior view.

Saddle Cabinet cont'd

10. Hang the doors using three cabinet hinges apiece, following the manufacturer's directions. (Note: Don't use screws that are longer than ½ inch, or you risk penetrating all the way through the plywood. We used #10 ½-inch wood screws.) Use a level to double-check that the doors are level and plumb.

11. Sand and finish the exterior and interior of the project. Sanding the plywood will remove the manufacturer's printing or any other unsightly surface blemishes. Finishing adds depth of color, shine, and durability.

Option

Add small side shelves using 1x6 boards and shelf brackets along the right side of the cabinet, as desired. Install up to four bridle brackets on the left side. We also added a few smaller hooks below the shelf on the right side for helmets, spurs, crops, and chaps, and hooks on the back of one door for girths. Add door handles and a hasp and lock to the outside of the doors.

This interior view shows the placement of the saddle racks, bridle brackets, and shelves.

Add Molding for a Finished Look

Prefabricated molding is inexpensive and readily available. We decided to install 1-inch coved molding in the panels of our cabinet doors to give the cabinet a more finished look. To do this, simply measure and cut eight mitered pieces $11\frac{7}{8}$ inches long for the horizontal spaces of the panels and eight mitered pieces 60 inches long for the vertical spaces of the panels. Align them in the inner frames of the 1x3 panels and attach them to the lx3s using $1\frac{1}{4}$-inch brad nails.

Close-up of the corner miter joint of the molding, in place against the 1x3 trim.

Wall-Mounted Whip Holder

Difficulty Rating: ∩ ∩

This whip holder is so easy to make, everyone should have one or two in the tack room. It is constructed from two small scraps of wood, which you can scavenge for free from other projects. Alternatively, you can buy exotic wood and make this into a real art piece. It will keep your delicate whips and crops organized, preventing the ends from becoming frayed by resting on the floor. Our whip holder accommodates thirteen whips, which is a lot of whips. We designed our whip holder to be installed on the side of the saddle cabinet described above. If your needs are more minimal, simply construct the holder using smaller dimensions and fewer holes.

Wall-Mounted Whip Holder

Tools

- Table saw or handsaw
- Router and round-over bit
- Drill with ¾-inch multipurpose bit
- Jigsaw
- Screw gun
- #10 tapered countersink bit
- Two 12-inch bar clamps

Materials

- Two scraps of wood, such as 2x6s, that each measure 30 inches long
- #10 2-inch screws

Building the Whip Holder

1. Our whip holder is 30 inches long by 6 inches deep, accommodating thirteen whips. The crescent-shaped 2x6 board functions as the whip holder shelf, while the straight 2x6 serves as a backing board that attaches to the saddle cabinet (or wall). Start by cutting the 2x6s to the desired length using a saw. Then, draw a crescent onto one of the 2x6s. Secure the board to a work space using bar clamps and cut the crescent shape using a jigsaw.

2. Measure and mark a point 3 inches in from both the left and right sides on the crescent-shaped 2x6 (see diagram). Then, measure and mark points at 2-inch increments between these two marks. Next, use a speed square to draw lines at each mark that extend to the curved front of the board. These lines show the locations of the whip holders. Last, measure 2 inches in from the crescent side along each line and mark with an "X."

3. Drill initial holes. First, use the bar clamps to secure the crescent 2x6 to a work surface, with the front edge overhanging by several

inches. (Insert a piece of scrap wood under it to prevent the wood from splintering and "blowing out" when you drill through it; a piece of plywood works best.) Next, use a drill with a ¾-inch multipurpose drill bit to make holes at each marked "X."

4. Cut the remaining wood to establish the whip holders. Use a jigsaw to saw through the crescent front of the board, meeting the edges of each hole (see photos).

5. Use a router with a round-over bit to bevel the edges of the top and bottom sides of the crescent front, including the inside edges of each hole.

6. Attach the backing board 2x6 to the crescent-shaped 2x6. On a flat work space, align the backing board perpendicularly to the front. Predrill and countersink pilot holes first, drilling through the back of the backing board into the flat edge of the crescent-shaped board. Use 2-inch screws to secure the boards together.

7. If desired, apply a coat of paint or stain and polyurethane.

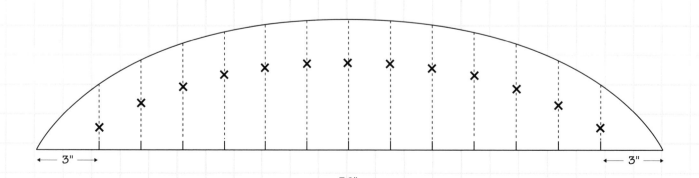

Use a jigsaw to cut into the wood.

Top view, with one hole yet to be cut (far right).

8. Predrill and countersink two mounting holes approximately 2 inches down from the top and 2 inches in from the sides of the backing board. Screw the whip holder to the wall using 2-inch screws.

9. Hang whips by inserting them through the holes, tip down.

Option

Since the size of this piece is so small, it isn't too expensive to experiment with exotic wood. Instead of basic pine, look for scraps of tiger-eye maple, mahogany, or purpleheart in the discount pile at a woodworking supply store. If you're really creative, use a router or jigsaw to cut the piece into an interesting organic shape, rather than just a rectangle or crescent. Use your imagination!

CHAPTER 4

Horse Housing

The stables are the real center of the household.
—George Bernard Shaw, *Heartbreak House*

The projects in this section are the largest and most difficult in the book. They require a more advanced skill set, demand the use of power tools, can be time-consuming, in some cases require the assistance of more than one person, and are generally not appropriate for children's participation. However, they are also the projects that can potentially save you the most money.

For example, we built our lean-to for less than $1,000 in materials. The same shed would likely cost several thousand dollars if constructed by a contractor. A prefabricated stall door purchased from a manufacturer costs up to $500, but we built ours for less than $100 in materials.

For all the projects in this chapter, the best lumber to use is rough-sawn. We used hemlock, since it is the most cost-effective in our area (the Northeast), but in other regions, different native species may be less expensive.

A Formula for Sawhorses Built to Work

Difficulty Rating: ∩ ∩ ∩

There's nothing more frustrating and self-defeating than when cheap, store-bought plastic sawhorses jiggle and collapse under you just when you are about to make the first cut in a 14-foot 2x8. A good set of sawhorses is a must for anyone who is taking on a building project. And building the sawhorses helps one to learn good crafting techniques that apply to other projects. The sawhorses we built were used while making the wooden projects in this book, both in this chapter and in the Tack Room and Jumps chapters. These instructions describe how to make one sawhorse. To be effective and useful, you'll need to make at least two.

Now, one can easily buy prefabricated heavy-duty sawhorses—but where's the fun in that? We encourage you to comb the countryside, the backyards and garages of relatives and friends, as well as your own scrap piles to find wood that can be shaped into the parts of a sawhorse. In this manner, you will save yourself a bundle, have something to be proud of and to be proud to work on, and learn how to create something that didn't exist before but has a real purpose: to work for you. The lumber for our sawhorses came from a relative's deck-building scrap and reject pile. Instead of becoming unwanted waste, the pressure-treated $^5/_4$ boards and 2x6 decking boards were saved. You might find boards of a different size and type. Therefore, the instructions below mainly identify and describe the parts of a sawhorse, how to make them, and how to assemble them. You can follow the formula while using different-sized lumber, such as 2x4s for legs instead of $^5/_4$ board.

Sawhorse

Tools

- Table saw
- Miter saw or miter box and handsaw
- Drill and #10 tapered predrill and countersink bit
- Screw gun
- Level
- Measuring tape
- Speed square
- Two 12-inch bar clamps
- Two 4-foot pipe clamps

Materials (for one sawhorse)

- Two 36-inch-long 2x6 boards
- Four ⁵⁄₄, 2x4, or 2x6 boards that measure at least 30 to 32 inches
- Four ⁵⁄₄, 2x4, or 2x6 boards that measure at least 16 inches
- Two pieces of ¾-inch plywood that measure 12 inches x 12 inches square
- #10 2½-inch and 3-inch screws

Making and Assembling the Parts

1. Make the top board. To make the top, use one 36-inch-long 2x6. Using a table saw, cut the edges of the 2x6 at 15-degree angles.

Trace the ends of the sawhorse onto plywood to ensure the correct angle.

2. Make four legs. Cut the legs to the desired height. We cut our legs at 32 inches. To be joined with the top properly, the legs need opposite 15-degree mitered tops and bottoms. Use a miter saw or circular saw to make these cuts. The mitered tops enable the sawhorse to have a flat surface. The mitered bottoms enable the sawhorse to stand flat on the ground.

3. Attach the legs to the top. Secure the 2x6 top facedown on a work surface using 12-inch bar clamps. Align the legs so that they fit flush against the angled sides of the 2x6 top. Predrill

pilot holes and attach the legs using #10 2½-inch screws.

4. Construct two plywood leg braces. The leg braces have 15-degree angled sides that form a trapezoid (which is a four-sided polygon having exactly one pair of parallel sides) and are attached to each end of the sawhorse. The top dimension of each leg brace on our sawhorse is 6⅜ inches, which we determined by measuring the top surface of the sawhorse once the legs were attached to the top. To make your leg braces, miter-cut the two ¾-inch pieces of 12x12-square plywood at a 15-degree angle so that the top measurement equals the measurement of the top of your sawhorse.

5. Attach the plywood leg braces. First, secure the leg braces to each end of the sawhorse using 4-foot pipe clamps, making sure that the 15-degree angles of the legs and braces are aligned. Use a drill to predrill pilot holes and countersink. Attach the leg braces using #10 2½-inch screws.

6. Make four cross-members that have 15-degree mitered edges. These cross-members are attached halfway down each pair of legs, with one attached on the outside and one attached on the inside of each pair of legs. To determine the length of your cross-members, measure the distance from the center of one leg to the center of the leg facing opposite. Use a 12-inch bar clamp on each end to secure opposite-facing cross-members. Make sure that the 15-degree

angles align. Check with a level to see if the cross-members are straight. Predrill pilot holes and attach using #10 2½-inch screws.

7. Build and attach the shelf. The shelf is attached on top of the cross-members attached to the inside legs. The shelf is measured and cut to fit exactly between the inside legs. Once you've inserted your top into the sawhorse, predrill pilot holes and attach it to the cross-members using #10 2½-inch screws.

8. Turn the sawhorse right side up and place it on a flat, level surface. Test it using a carpenter's level, and try to wobble it. If it's not level, or unsteady in any way, turn it back over and drive two 3-inch screws into the bottom of the shortest leg. Adjust them until the sawhorse will stand level. An additional benefit is that if you have to work on an uneven surface such as a driveway, you can back the screws out or drive them in further as needed to create a level surface on top of the sawhorse.

Pole Shed

Difficulty Rating: ∩ ∩ ∩ ∩ ∩

A pole shed is simply a shed that is constructed using native, unmilled logs in place of framing lumber. If you have a lot of trees and want to save some money, a pole shed is a great option. Tom used black locust trees for his shed, since the wood is hard and resists rot. Cedar is another common wood that is naturally rot-resistant. In Maine, where we live, locust is not a native species. We

> The Pole Shed project is adapted from "Ponder a Pole Barn" by Tom Moates, originally published in *Natural Horse* magazine. Many thanks to Tom for the contribution of his expertise and photos! (www.tommoates.com)

have plenty of spruce, hemlock, and Douglas fir in our forest, which all rot within a few years when in contact with the ground. If you are not blessed with a naturally rot-resistant tree species, you will need to add the extra step of setting concrete footings to protect your posts from ground contact. (See the Lean-To Shed project for instructions on setting footings.)

When harvesting poles, try to find ones as straight as possible. Whenever using them for horizontal positions or rafters, they should be crowned. Crowning is eyeing down the pole to find the natural curve present in it, and then placing this curve upward. For reasons of strength, a framing member crowned up will tend to stay strong and only flatten to the effects of gravity, where one crowned down tends to be pulled increasingly toward that center valley, exacerbating the bend.

If you have ever built anything with conventional kiln-dried, properly dimensioned lumber and other various building supplies of superior dimensional consistency, get yourself a cup of chamomile tea now and accept that "square," "plumb," and "straight" are relative terms in the world of pole construction. This inherent inconsistency is not a huge deal when one gets as close as possible to straight, square, and plumb and combines that gallant effort with coverings that are somewhat forgiving.

Framing with poles can save hundreds of dollars in lumber costs; plus, the structure can go up quickly, and it looks appealing in a rustic way. Coping with the dimensional inconsistencies is the main issue to overcome, but with a little patience, a good eye, and some sharp tools, it doesn't take long to get the swing of it.

Pole Shed

Tools

- Chain saw or bow saw
- Air compressor with framing nailer, or hammer and decking spikes
- Level
- Posthole digger and shovel
- Ax and/or draw knife

Materials

- A selection of long, straight, slender, rot-resistant trees
- Siding material such as wide white-pine boards
- Prefab metal roofing
- Concrete (optional, depending on wood species and climate)
- Decking spikes

Building the Pole Shed

1. Choose a site for your shed that is as flat, level, and well-drained as possible.
2. Select and harvest your poles. Find trees that are approximately 8 to 10 inches in diameter at the base, and as straight and long as possible. Cut them down using a chain saw or bow saw, and trim off all the branches and twigs. Removing the bark with an ax or draw knife reduces the risk of bugs or rot setting in, particularly in the underground area of the post. Trim the posts to the desired length, remembering to add 3 feet of length to any post that will be set into the ground.
3. Layout for a pole building is like any other. Get a measuring tape and mark out your corners. Make certain to measure to the outside of the post edges, and mark the corners first. Use stakes to mark the outer point of the corners, making sure that the distance between each post is correct, and double-check for squareness by pulling the diagonal measurements between opposing corners—the diagonals will be the same if the layout is square.
4. Once the corners are marked, get out the posthole digger and dig holes large enough to accommodate the diameter of your posts and at least 3 feet deep. If you require intermittent posts, set the corners first, then run a string line around the outer edge of the corners to determine the exact placement of the others.
5. Set the posts into the holes. Use a 4-foot level laid upright alongside the posts to check that they are plumb. Tom just tamps dirt and rocks into the holes to set them, using a small, pointed tamp stick, like the end of a shovel

handle, with many small shovelfuls of fill put into the hole around the post between tampings. (Note: If your climate is very damp or the wood species is prone to rot, you should set concrete footings for the posts rather than setting them directly into the soil. See Lean-To Shed project for instructions on setting concrete footings. Remember that when you use this method, the posts can be cut 3 feet shorter, since they don't need to be sunk into the ground.)

6. With the posts all tamped in and relatively plumb, choose some thinner poles long enough to stretch between them horizontally at the top, middle, and bottom. These will serve as nailers for your siding and will tie the structure around the perimeter. At the ground level, use black locust or other rot-resistant species. (If you don't have access to such a species, it may be better in the long run to invest in some pressure-treated lumber for the bottom nailers.)

   The shed requires bottom, middle, and top nailers with the short side averaging 8 feet tall and the higher side at around 12 feet. The top cross-poles on these two sides not only serve as nailers, but they also carry the load of the rafters, so size them up a bit from typical nailer posts and choose strong hardwoods, such as white oak or hickory. These cross-poles will be notched into the posts and spiked in place with long galvanized decking spikes.

7. Hold the top cross-pole against the posts where it needs to be permanently positioned. Getting generally level here is a good idea as well. A string line with a small level attached

There are three horizontal nailers on each wall, at the top, middle, and bottom.

Notice the notch at the top of the post, which receives the notched end of the header.

can help to get the poles level around the shed. Establish the post tops this way, mark them, and then cut the tops with a chain saw to establish the level roofline that is defined by the uppermost horizontal poles. Mark where the notching should be on both the post and the cross-piece.

8. Notch the vertical posts and horizontal poles so they fit together. With a combination of saw, ax, and perhaps chisel, remove half the wood from the post and half from the pole so that ultimately, the pole ends up flush. When complete, the two should slide into one another. Drive a couple of decking spikes through the pole into the post to secure the joint.

9. At this point, if the pole is really straight and you have recessed the notches so the outer surface of the cross-pole is flush with the outer surface of the post, you are in good shape for siding. Often, though, the cross-poles and/or

the posts are a little squirrelly. In this instance you can nail the cross-pole in place and then rip whatever wayward edges exist with a chain saw or an ax, to flush out the surface that will receive the siding. Simply sight down along the pole in question and your eye will clearly see large discrepancies in need of adjusting. If such a pole must be positioned where it curves too far to the interior of the building, you may rip a board to fill in the troubling spot and nail it along the pole or post, thereby filling it out to flush.

10. Next select, lay out, and notch the rafters, spaced on 3-foot centers. Be sure to crown them. The notches in rafters—where they set onto the top wall poles (called "bird's mouths" in carpentry)—should be kept shallow, as you want to retain as much structural integrity as possible. Flattening out the spots where they rest on the cross-pole provides a stable spot for

Pole Shed cont'd

This view shows several elements, including the rafters, one purlin, the metal roofing, and the siding.

the bird's mouths to fit onto, but don't notch here in the half-and-half deep fashion as on the siding nailers. If you position the end rafters at the building's edge, flush with the horizontal poles below, they can act both as rafters and the top nailer for the siding. A single spike driven down through the rafter pole into the pole below at each notch should suffice to anchor them.

11. Metal roofing is my preference for pole structures. It easily covers the inconsistencies of the rough poles while still looking good. For this type of roofing, 1x3 purlins (onto which the metal roof will later be attached) are nailed on 2-foot centers across the length of the roof perpendicular to the rafters, with a couple of 12d nails at each rafter intersection. If you run the purlins well beyond the roof's edge, then you can pop a chalk line and trim just where the edge needs to be. You can have whatever overhang you prefer, and you can square out the roof exactly, even if the inconsistency from the poles plagued you at the rafter level. Then the metal roofing can go on per the manufacturer's instructions.

12. Vertical siding is a good choice, and wide white-pine boards go up quickly and cover well. Other siding types, such as metal or horizontal board, also can work. With any siding, just keep an eye out for how the project is progressing, stepping back occasionally to sight the wall. Make adjustments by trimming or filling out as needed. Apply siding to the back and sides of the shed, leaving the front open.

Lean-To Shed

Difficulty Rating: ∩ ∩ ∩ ∩ ∩

Building a shed that will be attached to an existing building—known as a lean-to—is a rather large undertaking and will require the assistance of two to three people. It is also a good idea to check with your local zoning board to determine whether you will be required to obtain building permits. Adding to an existing building may also add to your property taxes and homeowner's insurance.

Nevertheless, a lean-to is rewarding to build and has many benefits. It can be used for storage of hay, wood, farm equipment, or vehicles. It can also be used as a shelter for animals. We use our large, 12x30 shed as a rain shelter and to provide shade for our horses. A metal gate divides the shelter into two sides so that the lower-ranking horses can be safe in their own side of the shed. To house horses, ideally each horse should have a minimum of 12 feet by 12 feet of space.

These instructions are for a 12-foot-deep, 30-foot-long shed with a roof that is 12 feet high where it meets the side of our barn, and 8 feet high at the front edge. Be sure to adjust the measurements as needed to fit your existing structure and your needs. The first step to this structure is to plan it. Before buying materials, measure the existing structure and sketch out a site plan.

Master Craftsman Lives Next Door
We built our lean-to shed with the generous help of our industrious neighbor, Bill Moriarty. Bill has been building houses, sheds, decks, and stairs for over forty years. He is a true do-it-yourselfer, a superior craftsman, an excellent mentor, and an untiring worker. When we moved to Maine, we didn't know what or who we would find. Bill's friendship has been one of the best aspects of our life here. Without him, who knows what would have become of us (and our barn).

Lean-To Shed

Tools

- Circular saw
- Drill with a ½-inch bit and a ⅛-inch bit
- Screw gun with a ¼-inch socket bit to match the metal roofing screws
- Impact driver or socket wrench
- Air compressor and framing nail gun (or hammer)
- Laser level
- Handsaw
- Reciprocating saw
- Measuring tapes
- Hammer
- Framing square
- Level
- Shovel
- Quick square
- Chalk line
- Cement mixer or wheelbarrow
- Trowel
- Hose
- Two to three sawhorses
- Tin snips

Materials

- Three 4-foot-long, 10-inch-diameter cylindrical concrete forms (Sono tubes)
- Six to eight 80-pound bags of concrete mix
- Eight 14-foot 2x8s (header and gable ends)
- 224 linear feet of 1x4 (purlins)
- Three 10-foot 4x6s (posts)
- Two 16-foot 4x6s (headers)
- Fifteen 14-foot 2x6s (rafters)
- Two 16-foot 1x6s (fascia)
- One 8-foot 4x6 (to be cut into gussets)
- Thirty-six 5½-inch lag screws
- Ten 3-foot-wide-by-14-foot-long strips of prefab metal roofing
- Three 10-foot, 6-inch pieces of metal roof flashing
- 400 matching metal roofing screws
- 3½-inch nails for the framing nailer
- Six pieces of 4-inch-long angle iron
- Twelve 2½-inch tapered wood screws
- Six 3-inch concrete expansion screws

Making the Shed

1. Make a site plan (see chapter introduction). Make sure that the surface is level and well drained. Ideally, remove the topsoil and replace it with hardpan, gravel, or sand.
2. Measure the approximate locations of the corner posts and center post, and dig a hole 4 feet deep by 12 inches wide at each point.
3. Use batter boards and strings to lay out the plan. Fix a set of batter boards at each corner, approximately 2 feet out from where the actual corner posts of the lean-to will be (see diagram). The corner posts need to be square with the outer edges of the existing structure, and with each other. The strings allow you to eyeball what's square. First, attach a string to the left corner of the building. Walk away from the building, past the batter boards, holding the string taut. Move the string to the right

A Note about Digging Holes

Let's be realistic: Digging holes for footings that will support a heavy structure can be extremely difficult depending on the soil type. Luckily, our neighbor Whitey has a 7½-foot backhoe. We started digging by hand using a shovel and posthole digger, and within about 12 inches into the first hole, we hit large rocks that were impossible to move by hand. We decided to call Whitey. For a small fee, Whitey was able to use his backhoe to dig the three holes for our footings deep enough to get below the frost line within an hour. To dig these three holes by hand would have required at least a week, as well as some serious digging tools such as a long breaker bar to break up clay and to leverage rock.

   If your area has hard or rocky soil, we recommend either becoming friendly with your neighbors or hiring someone to come dig the holes for you. This will add to your cost, but will be a saving grace in the long run, both for your back and for the life of the structure.

until you see it bend at the corner of the building. Move it back to the left until the bend disappears. The string is now square to the side of the building. Tie the string to the batter board at this point, using a nail or screw to hold it in place. Repeat this process on the other side. The two strings represent the outer edges of the corner posts.

Now you need to determine the front edge of the corner posts. We measured 12 feet, 6 inches from the edge of the building along each string, and marked these points with a marking pen. We then ran a third piece of string between the other two batter boards such that it crossed the first two strings at the marked points. We then used a framing square between the intersecting strings to double-check our work. Measure the diagonals as a final check. The length of the two diagonals should be exactly the same.

Place the tube into the hole and secure it with a few shovelfuls of soil.

Batter boards with strings mark the location for the Sono tube. (The cross-point of the strings is actually lined up over the hole. The angle of the photo makes it appear otherwise.)

Place an upturned bucket over the tube to prevent accidentally throwing soil into the tube as you fill the hole.

4. Preparing the footings: Place a 4-foot section of tubing in each hole. Use a level on two opposite sides of the tubing to ensure that the tubing is plumb. Carefully, fill around the bottom edges and recheck with your level.

    Once the tubing is secure, fill the hole completely until only 2 inches of tubing remains above the ground.

5. Now, mix and fill each section of tubing with concrete. Level the surface of the concrete at the top of each footing using a 2x4. This is known as screeding. Allow the concrete to cure for two days. If concrete is exposed to direct sunlight, cover it with a wet towel and keep it moist to prevent the top from drying too quickly, which could cause a crack.

Lean-To Shed cont'd

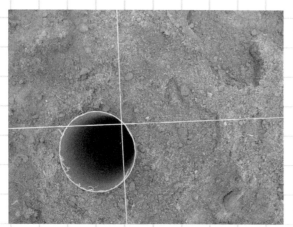

The strings, here clearly marking the eventual location of the outer edges of the post.

6. Preparing and setting the posts: Cut each end of the 4x6 posts so they are square. Cut the first post to the correct height according to the site plan. Since the concrete footings will inevitably be at varying heights, use a laser level to determine the required height of the remaining posts based on the height of the first post (see sidebar). Measure, square, and cut the remaining posts. Set them on the appropriate footings and brace them with 2x4s.

Attach the posts to the concrete footers using concrete screws and purpose-made brackets or simple strips of angle iron, as shown here. Use an impact driver to drive the screws into the concrete.

7. When all your posts are set, it is time to put up the header. We used a 4x6 header placed on top of the posts in post-and-lintel style. Using

Using a Laser Level

Use a long tape measure or transit measuring stick. Extend the measuring tape from the center of each footing upward until it meets the light from the laser level. This gives you the height of that post and compensates for any slope that may exist.

3½-inch framing nails or screws, secure the header to the posts by using 4-inch-by-8-inch plywood braces. The braces overlap the header by 4 inches and overlap the post by 4 inches.

The posts and header are now in place. The crossed 2x4s are there to support the posts until the structure is complete. They will be removed later.

8. The next step requires that you determine the height of your ledger and secure it to the wall of the existing building. We used a 2x8 board for our ledger. First, we removed the batten boards on our barn wall to create a flush surface for the ledger. Then, we measured and marked the height of the top of the ledger on the left side of the barn wall. Use a stud finder to locate the wall studs, and mark their position. Now, raise the top of the left side of the ledger to the height mark you made on the wall earlier, as the top of the ledger board is the roofline. Attach the ledger initially with one 3½-inch nail. Next, raise the right side of the ledger and use a level to determine the correct height. When the right side is level, attach

with a 3½-inch nail. To secure the ledger, use 5-inch lag screws with washers. Fasten a lag screw to every other stud.

9. Preparing the rafters: Keep in mind that the length of the rafters will determine the depth of the roof overhang. Also, you need to take into account the pitch of the roof; if the shed is 12 feet deep, the rafters need to be longer than 12 feet. (See the discussion of site planning in the chapter introduction.) Make sure that you have determined how each rafter board crowns and face them all in the same direction, which we call "making them all frown."

10. It is now time to cut the rafters. Since the shed measures 12 feet, 6 inches wide, 14-foot 2x6 lumber is sufficient length for rafters, including a small overhang. Therefore, after double-checking to make sure each board is truly 14 feet, simply make the plumb cuts on each end, saving the effort of calculating a precise rafter length and overhang. The only critical length measurement is to accurately locate the bird's-mouth cut for each rafter.

Establish Rafter Direction

First, determine the crown of each 14-foot 2x6. The crown is the natural direction the wood bows. It is important that all the rafters crown in the same direction—i.e., they should all "frown"—to ensure the rigidity of the roof. To see the crown, lay each board on a pair of sawhorses, tip the board on edge, and sight down the length.

The Wonderful World of Roofs and Rafters

Rafters require three important cuts: One is called a bird's-mouth cut, which enables the rafter to rest level with the header; the second is called the top plumb cut, which will be secured to the side of the ledger; the third is the bottom plumb cut, which allows the front of the roof to be square. Each of the cuts is determined relative to the pitch of the structure's roof. We decided to use what is called a 5-pitch, as this is appropriate for a metal roof given the weather in Maine—meaning the pitch is steep enough to allow the sun and gravity to prevent snow from accumulating on the roof. Rafters are angled to frame the pitch of a roof. Roof pitch is measured as rise over span. In our case, "5:12 pitch" means 5 inches of rise occurs over 12 inches of span; essentially, the greater the first number, the greater the pitch.

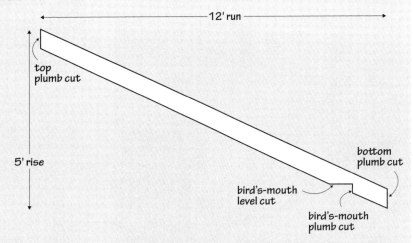

Lean-To Shed cont'd

This board crowns toward the left.

Once you've organized your rafter boards in the same direction, cut and test one rafter to serve as a template for the rest.

Make Wall Plumb Cut

The wall plumb cut is made on the end of the rafter that will be attached to the ledger board on the wall of the main structure, as it creates the angle of the roof, known as the pitch. We used a 5:12 pitch for our roof. Use a framing square to mark the angle of the wall plumb cut. To do so, align the outside 5-inch mark of the tongue (the narrow arm of the framing square) on the top of one end of the 2x6, and align the outside 12-inch mark of the blade

Mark the wall plumb cut along the outside edge of the tongue.

(the wider arm of the square) along the top edge of the 2x6. Draw a line along the outside edge of the tongue. This line indicates the wall plumb cut for the rafter. Make your cut using a circular saw.

Make the Face Plumb Cut

The face plumb cut is made on the other end of the rafter, opposite from the wall plumb cut. Simply reverse the square and repeat the process you followed for the wall plumb cut, only this time align the outside 5-inch mark of the tongue and the outside 12-inch mark of the blade on the bottom side of the 2x6 (i.e., the underside of the crown). Draw a line on the outside of the tongue to mark the angle. This line indicates the face plumb cut for the rafter. Make your cut using a circular saw.

Flip the square over to mark the face plumb cut along the outside edge of the tongue.

Make the Bird's-Mouth Cuts

The bird's mouth of a rafter consists of two cuts: one level cut to enable the rafter to sit square on the top of the header, and one plumb cut to allow the rafter to "hook" flush with the front of the header.

To make the bird's-mouth plumb cut, following our dimensions, measure 14⅞ inches back along the bottom side of the rafter starting from the bottom edge of the face plumb cut. Mark the measurement clearly. Then, align the outside 5-inch mark of the tongue of the framing square on the 14⅞-inch measurement and align the outside 12-inch mark of the blade on the bottom side of the 2x6. Draw

Bird's-mouth plumb cut.

Bird's-mouth level cut.

a line on the outside of the tongue across the 2x6 at this point. This line marks the plumb cut of the bird's mouth.

Before cutting the bird's-mouth plumb cut line, you also need to mark the bird's-mouth level cut

These marks indicate the location of the cuts for the bird's mouth.

and square it with the bird's-mouth plumb cut. To do so, realign the outside of the tongue to the bird's-mouth plumb cut line and use the outside of the blade to measure for the thickness of your header. In our case, the rough cut header is 4 inches thick, so the level cut is marked at 4 inches. Make a line from the edge of the 2x6 along the outside of the blade until it connects with the plumb cut line of the bird's mouth. (Note: The length of the bird's-mouth plumb cut is 1½ inches.)

Use a circular saw to start the cuts, being careful not to over-cut. Finish the cuts using a handsaw.

11. Installing the rafters comes next. (Note: To ensure proper installation, it is important that there are at least two people available during this step.) First, it is best to measure and mark lines on both your ledger and on your header to indicate the placement of each rafter. On our project, we placed rafters 2 feet apart on the center. This meant that we marked our first lines at 25 inches, and from this mark, we measured and made additional lines every 24 inches. We installed each of the rafters to the right of lines.

Lean-To Shed cont'd

The three posts, the header, and most of the rafters are now installed. The braces are still in place to support the structure.

We recommend toe-nailing the rafters to the header on the bottom plumb cut end first, and then toe-nailing the top plumb cut end to the ledger on the wall of the existing building. If the existing structure's outside wall is not exactly straight, the person on the header end of the structure may need to lean on the header to help the plumb end reach the ledger. If the building is bowed severely, use a 2x4 angled against the header to provide extra leverage (see photo).

Here Bill uses an extra 2x4 to push the header, forcing the rafters as tightly as possible against the ledger, while Jason secures them.

12. Cutting and attaching the purlins: Run the first 1x4 purlin along the top of the roof, butting up against the existing building on the ledger. Starting at the top of the first purlin, measure

A Note on Joist Hangers and Toe-Nailing

Joist hangers are commonly used to secure rafters when a roof is built with S4S lumber. As we used rough lumber, we found that joist hangers were too small, so we toe-nailed the rafters instead. Toe-nailing is driving a nail at an angle through one board into another to join the two together. Our neighbor, Bill, who aided in the design and construction of our shed, believes that toe-nailing is a more efficient way to secure rafters. He has forty years of experience in the home-building industry, so we took him at his word.

Toe-nailing the rafters to the ledger board.

2-foot increments from the top of the roof down, and snap a chalk line across the rafters at each point. Each chalk line represents the top edge of a purlin. The last purlin should be placed right at the ends of the rafters, even if that point falls at less than 2 feet. We bought our purlins wholesale, so they came in linear feet, meaning that each board was not the exact same length. This was so that we could stagger the joints of the purlins along the length of the roof, adding to the integrity of the roof. Attach the purlins using 2-inch nails.

A view of the rafters and purlins from below. In the foreground, you can also see the lap joint between the two long boards that form the header.

13. Preparing the metal roofing: Metal roofing comes without predrilled holes for the screws. You need to predrill holes in all but one of the panels such that when the roofing is installed, the holes will line up with the purlins, preventing damage to the roofing material when you screw them down. Measure 2 inches down from the top of the roofing, and snap a chalk line at that point. From that first line, measure and snap a chalk line every 2 feet. Using a ⅛-inch drill bit, drill pilot holes for the screws along these chalk lines approximately every 8 inches. You should be able to drill through three sheets of roofing at once. (Note: Don't predrill holes in the last sheet, as you will need to overlap the last panel with the others so that it creates the correct overhang.)

14. Attaching the metal roofing: Install the first panel so that the finished edge overhangs the end rafter by approximately 2 inches. If your measurements are correct, the bottom edge of the panel should overhang the front of the rafters by at least 2 inches. Fasten the panel to the purlins with the roofing screws through the predrilled holes (the predrilled holes should align with the purlins). Install the subsequent panels, overlapping the edges of each panel according to the manufacturer's instructions. When you get to the final panel, use the sheet that you did not predrill. Rotate it 180 degrees from the others, so that when you install it on the roof, the finished side will overhang the gable end. Place it so that the finished edge overhangs the final rafter by 2 inches. This may require you to overlap the previous panel by quite a bit, which is why you did not predrill the pilot holes. You may need to remove previously installed screws when trying to overlap the last panel. Once you have determined the overlap, attach the last panel by bearing down on the screws so they penetrate the metal. Go slow so the screws do not slip and scratch the surface of the roofing.

15. Attaching the flashing: Ask the building supply store to bend the flashing to match the pitch of the roof. Fasten the flashing to the uppermost purlin, holding the back of it flush against the side of the existing building. Using the roofing screws, screw the flashing into the ribs of the

Attaching the flashing to cover the inevitable gap between the wall and the roof.

Lean-To Shed cont'd

metal roof (not the flat surface) approximately 1 inch from the edge of the flashing. To prevent leaks, you may choose to caulk the edge that contacts the existing building. If so, use clear exterior latex caulking.

16. Cutting and attaching support gussets on the posts: Gussets are braces that help stabilize the posts. Our lean-to had three posts. Each post received two gussets, which are the same lumber thickness as the posts and header, and they have mitered 45-degree angles so that they form right triangles with the header and post. The longer the span between the posts, the longer the hypotenuse (long side) of the right triangle needs to be. The length of the hypotenuse of our gussets measured 25 inches. We used our miter saw to cut 4x6s to length. We initially secured the gussets using the nail gun. We reinforced the joints by predrilling pilot holes for 5-inch lag screws. We used an impact driver to install the lag screws.

17. Installing a fascia board across the front of the rafters: We used ⅝x10 lumber to create a face board, known as a fascia, along the front of the lean-to just under the metal overhang. This board protects the end grain of the rafters from the elements and allows the option of installing gutters. Obviously, we did not use one continuous board to cover the 30-foot span of our lean-to; we used three 10-foot boards. We mitered the ends at 45-degree angles, using a circular saw, to enable the boards to overlap with each other.

Two gussets on a post. Gussets help stabilize the attachment of the post to the header.

This angle shows the lag screws attaching the gusset to the header. The fascia is the board attached to the fronts of the rafters.

Option

These instructions result in a roof with one back wall. This provides plenty of shelter from your average rain, snow, and sun. But if your shed is to be the sole source of shelter for animals year-round, it also needs to have two side walls along the short sides to create a block against wind and windblown precipitation during severe weather. The long front side can remain open.

To install siding, attach three horizontal nailers across the top, middle, and bottom of the shed's sides, and use them to attach vertical wooden siding or prefabricated metal siding.

An interior view of the side wall, showing the three nailers and vertical siding.

Our finished shed includes a gable end on the roof (foreground), as well as a side wall on the north side to block winter winds. A kickboard of ¾-inch plywood along the bottoms of the walls would be a wise addition as well.

Barn Doors

Difficulty Rating: ∩ ∩

When we moved into our house, the doors on the barn were overhead garage doors. They were flimsy, noisy, unattractive, and didn't keep out the cold. Also, the overhead tracks cut down on headroom in the aisle. We decided to replace them with classic sliding wooden doors.

These instructions will make one 4½-foot-wide door. Our barn doorway is 9 feet wide, so we built two doors and mounted them so they slide apart. The hardware for sliding doors can be purchased at most home improvement supply stores. Another option would be to mount the doors on hinges instead of sliders. Hinges are less expensive, but require a lot of space around the door to allow it to swing. Sliders are much more convenient.

We used rough-cut 2x6 hemlock boards to construct our doors, and they are very heavy and thick. However, the 2x6 lumber was pretty pricey. Doors constructed of ⁵⁄₄ board would be sufficiently sturdy, lighter in weight, and somewhat less expensive (⁵⁄₄ board is rough-cut lumber that is 1¼ inches thick). If you plan to paint or stain the doors, use planed lumber instead of rough-cut—but be sure to take into account the size difference between planed and rough-cut lumber in your measurements (see page 14).

Barn Doors

Tools

- Circular saw or miter saw
- Drill
- Screw gun
- 6-foot pipe clamps

Materials

- Nine 8-foot-long 2x6s (vertical boards)
- Three 4½-foot-long ⁵⁄₄x6s (cross-braces)
- Two 5-foot-long ⁵⁄₄x6s
- 3-inch screws
- Slider hardware kit
- 8-foot slider
- Lag screws
- Door handle

Building the Barn Door

1. Arrange the nine 8-foot 2x6s on a flat surface. Check to be sure they are square, and use the pipe clamps to hold them in place.
2. Align the three 4½-foot ⁵⁄₄x6s horizontally across the top, middle, and bottom of the 9-foot boards, as shown in the diagram. Predrill pilot holes, and use 2½-inch screws to attach the cross-braces. Make sure you have at least two screws in each vertical board.
3. Align one of the two 5-foot ⁵⁄₄x6s from corner to corner between the top and middle cross-braces. Use a straightedge to mark the angled cuts needed at the top and bottom. Use a miter saw to cut the angled ends. Predrill and screw the ⁵⁄₄x6 to the vertical boards. Repeat for the bottom piece.
4. Attach two slider rollers to the top of the door, following the instructions in the kit.
5. Attach an 8-foot header above the door opening, being sure to attach it to studs, not just to the wall. Mount the 8-foot slider to the header, according to the manufacturer's instructions.
6. Lift the door and slide it onto the sliders. (You will need at least two people for this job—the door is quite heavy.) Screw a wood scrap to each end of the slider to prevent the door from sliding off the ends.
7. Adjust the slider rollers so that the door hangs level, following the directions on the package.
8. Attach a handle to the door.

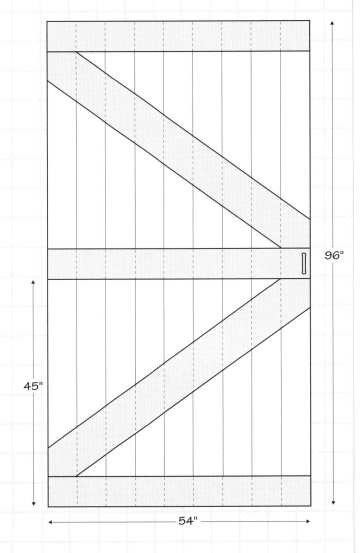

Barn Doors cont'd

Option

Before hanging the door, sand and paint or stain it using exterior paint or stain. A bright red door with white cross-braces is a classic look, or you can use your stable colors.

You can use any of several different patterns for the cross-braces. See below for some traditional patterns.

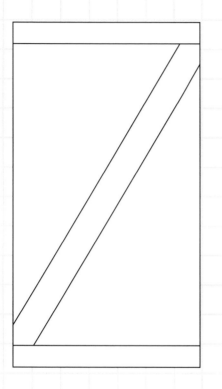

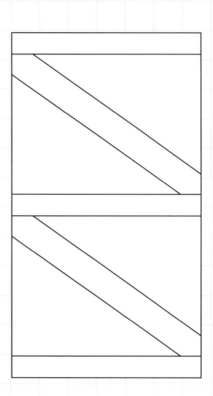

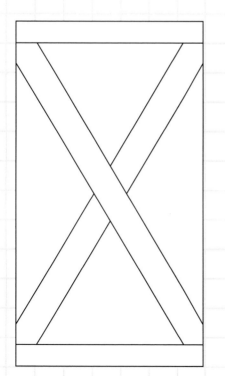

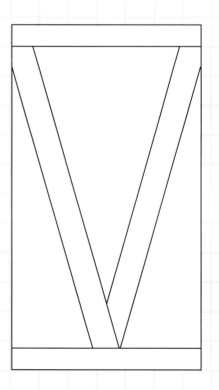

Wicked Rugged Maine Stall Doors

Difficulty Rating: ∩ ∩ ∩ ∩

The following project was inspired by the craftsmanship of Norman Justice Jr. of Gorham, Maine, and is written in memory of Margie Justice. Norm is a pretty rugged Mainah who single-handedly built sixteen horse stalls in an old dairy barn. The doors of each stall were impressive to us, given their heft, sturdiness, and quality of construction. They looked like professional doors. When finishing the stalls in our own barn, we decided to use Norm's stable door as the model. Norman's doors have rails and stiles, with an open-window top and a tongue-and-groove panel bottom.

The rails are the three horizontal members of the door, and the stiles are the two vertical members. These members frame the top window opening, provide a place to mount a latch in the middle, and create an area for the bottom panel. The stiles are 8-foot 2x6s, the top rail is a 4-foot 2x10, and the middle and bottom rails are 4-foot 2x6s.

It seems like it would be simple to overlap and screw the boards together at the top, middle, and the bottom. However, this would have resulted in an awkwardly thick door with inconsistent front and back dimensions. We would not have been able to hang the door using standard hardware, and the door would not have had long-lasting structural integrity—i.e., ruggedness. So, we decided to borrow a technique used in timber framing, called dado or rabbet joints. Using this technique, the rails and stiles of our barn door were able to fit flush against each other, as it created structural joints while maintaining a flat surface.

The technique was a bit daunting at first, so we practiced making rabbets on scraps of 2x6, and we recommend that you do this as well. Once we got the hang of it, we completed the door relatively quickly. The rabbets made for easy assembly, since the door fit together like a puzzle. This project is one we are especially proud of. Not only does this project serve a quintessential function for our horses in our barn, but the doors themselves look great and complete the appearance of the barn.

Rugged Stall Doors

Tools

- Circular saw
- Table saw and/or radial arm saw
- Screw gun
- Pipe clamps and bar clamps
- 2-inch chisel and mallet
- Speed square
- Measuring tape

Materials

- Two 8-foot 2x6s (rough hemlock)
- Two 4-foot 2x6s (rough hemlock)
- One 4-foot 2x10 (rough hemlock)
- 8 pieces of 6-inch-wide-by-4-foot-long tongue-and-groove paneling, or ½-inch plywood with faux tongue-and-groove appearance
- One 54½-inch 1x4 (S4S)
- Two 25½-inch 1x4s (S4S)
- Sliders and tracks (Stanley)
- A manufactured window grill, 36 inches wide by 30½ inches tall, if desired

Making the Stall Doors

1. Rabbet the two stiles. There are three rabbets in each stile—a top, middle, and bottom rabbet. See the sidebar below, which explains the cutting technique we used. The rabbet cuts for the rails and stiles are ⅞ inches deep. The top rabbet is 10 inches long, measuring down from the top of the stiles. (Since we're using rough lumber, measure the exact width of the 2x10 rail, and use that measurement as the length of the top rabbet. Same goes for the rabbets that will receive the middle and bottom rails.) The middle rabbet is 6 inches long. To locate the middle rabbet, measure 39 inches down from the top of each stile and mark the measurement with a square; then, measure 45 inches down from the top and make another mark with a square. Cut a 6-inch rabbet between these marks for the middle rail. The bottom rabbet is also 6 inches long, measuring from the bottom up (see diagram).

2. Rabbet the rails, following the same cutting technique. See the sidebar. See diagram for rabbet measurements.

3. Make long, horizontal rabbet cuts on stiles and middle and bottom rails to receive tongue-and-groove panel (see diagram).

4. Assemble rails and stiles.

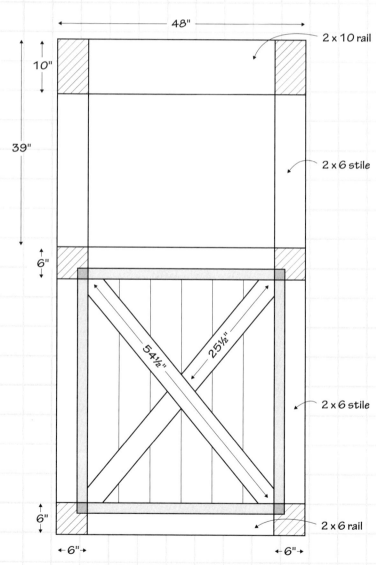

This photo shows the alignment of the three rails and one of the stiles. The top of the door is at right, and the bottom is at left.

Making Rabbet Cuts Using a Circular Saw

1. Secure a board to a workspace using a bar clamp. Measure and mark the width of the rabbet cut.

2. Adjust the cutting depth of your circular saw to $7/8$-inch. Make a series of cuts across the grain approximately $1/8$ to $1/4$ inch apart. Stop at mark.

Make cuts $1/4$ inch apart at a depth of $7/8$ inch.

3. Then, use a mallet to break free the remaining wood from between the cuts.

This is what the board looks like after making the cuts and before chiseling out the wood.

4. Last, use a chisel and mallet to remove remaining wood and to create a smooth receiving surface.

Use a chisel and mallet to remove the remaining wood and smooth the surface of the joint.

This is a rabbet that will fit together with a rabbet of another board to form a joint.

The finished rabbet cut.

(Note: You can use a table saw to achieve the same result. If the table saw has a dado blade, it will remove much more wood with each cut, so your work will be much more efficient and there will be no chiseling.)

Rugged Stall Doors cont'd

5. Make tongue-and-groove panel. The panel needs to measure 40½ inches wide and 40½ inches high in order to set into the framed space created by the rabbet cuts on the back of the stiles and the middle and bottom rails. Therefore, cut eight pieces of 6-inch-wide tongue-and-groove panel boards to length and fit together. You will need to trim the tongue off the final board in order to allow the panel to fit within the framed space.

6. Insert the panel into the space on the backside of the door. Use a 1⅝-inch screw through the top and bottom of each panel board to attach the panel to the rails. Also, use screws on the edge panel boards to attach the panel to the stiles.

7. Make the X for the panel. Measure and mark the center of each end of the 54½-inch 1x4. Starting from the mark, miter the edge of the boards at 45-degree angles to form a point on each end. Now, do the same for the two 25½-inch 1x4s; however, only make a point on one end of each board. Align the long 1x4 on the face of the panel so that the two points fit into the corners formed by the 2x6 frame of the rails and stiles. Predrill and screw the 1x4 into each panel board using 1⅝-inch screws. Finally, align the two shorter 1x4s on the face of the panel so that their points fit into the opposite corners formed by the 2x6s (see photo below).

8. Attach window grill following the manufacturer's instructions.

9. Install tracks and sliders according to directions provided with the hardware.

This is just one type of slider hardware. Refer to the instructions on your hardware's packaging to install it correctly.

10. Hang door. Check that it slides freely along the floor. If not, remove it and trim the bottom with hand planer or circular saw, and rehang. Finally, install a latch.

The finishing touch is to install a latch.

The panel, made of tongue-and-groove boards, fits into the frame created by the rails and stiles and is stabilized by the X.

CHAPTER 5

Jumps

A horse which stops dead just before a jump and thus propels its rider into a graceful arc provides a splendid excuse for general merriment.

—Prince Philip, Duke of Edinburgh

Purchasing jumps at retail is astonishingly expensive. A full course of show-quality jumps can cost tens of thousands of dollars. Even a few simple schooling jumps—constructed of plain standards, rails, and maybe a panel or flower box—can set you back several hundred dollars.

The only way to avoid this very large expense, yet still have an arena full of attractive and safe jumps, is to build them yourself. This chapter will help you build a variety of fences, including basic standards and wing standards, a picket gate, a flower box, a "brick" wall, a brush box, and a set of cavalletti. Each project costs less than a hundred dollars in materials, and takes just a few hours to build at most.

For our jumps, we used a uniform height of 5 feet for standards and 10 feet for the width of the jump. When designing your own course, you can choose to make the standards taller or shorter according to your needs. Jumps can vary in width from 8 feet to 12 feet.

Wood used in jump construction should always be pressure-treated. Pressure-treated wood is more expensive and heavier than untreated wood, but it will last years longer when exposed to precipitation and constant ground contact. Finish the jumps with white or colored exterior-grade stain or paint for an attractive appearance and added rot protection. First prime and then stain using oil-based primer and stain. We recommend Cabot's Problem-Solver oil-based primer and Cabot's latex solid color stain.

Lay out the boards on sawhorses. Using either a fine paintbrush or pneumatic spray gun, apply the primer first and let it dry for 24 hours. Once the boards have dried, apply the stain using the same method.

To complete the jumps, you will need several jump poles. You will not find a chapter here on how to make poles, since they are so simple. You have a variety of options. Pressure-treated 4x4s, 4-inch round posts, landscape timbers, and white PVC piping are all available in 8-, 10-, or 12-foot lengths, and all make functional jump poles. You could also cut straight, slender saplings into appropriate lengths to make a natural-looking jump.

If you use wood poles, simply finish them in white using exterior-grade stain or paint. You can also leave them natural, or paint colored stripes on the poles for a professional appearance. If using square 4x4 posts, it is best to chamfer the edges with a router or power sander, removing the 90-degree corners that would be painful to the horse if he hit them with his legs.

PVC piping is already white. Be sure to purchase a heavy-duty gauge for safety. Too-thin PVC can crack or break when stepped on by a horse, causing injury from the jagged shards.

Jump cups must be purchased from a catalog, online, or from a local tack shop. Prices range from $5 to $30. You can choose metal or plastic cups, and breakable pins are now available for added safety.

Cavalletti

Difficulty Rating: ∩ ∩

Cavalletti are low, adjustable-height jumps used for schooling the young horse or novice rider over fences. They can also be used as trotting or cantering poles, laid out in sequence and set at the lowest or middle height, to encourage the horse to move with greater cadence and impulsion. The Xs on the ends not only allow for height adjustment, but also prevent the poles from rolling across the ground should a horse knock one with a hoof. These cavalletti adjust to three heights: 6 inches, 12 inches, or 18 inches. You will want several cavalletti to create jumping grids or trotting pole sequences, so plan on making at least four of them.

The top photo shows the cavalletti at its full height of 18 inches. In the bottom photo, it is at the middle height of 12 inches.

The cavalletti at its lowest height of 6 inches.

Cavalletti

Tools

- Table saw, miter saw, or circular saw
- Hammer or nail gun and 3-inch nails
- Speed square
- Tape measure
- Drill with 1-inch recess bit and ¼-inch multipurpose bit
- Impact driver with ½-inch impact socket, or ½-inch socket and socket wrench

Materials

- Four 29½-inch-long 2x4s
- Two 14½-inch-long 2x4s
- Two 11½-inch-long 2x4s
- One 10-foot-long, 4-inch-diameter wood pole or landscape timber
- Four 4-inch lag screws with 1-inch diameter washers

Building the Cavalletti

1. Lay out the four 29½-inch 2x4s, and measure and mark them as shown in the diagram.
2. Set aside two of the marked 2x4s. Center one on top of the other using the marks as guides, forming an X-shape as shown. (The X will be uneven, with two legs longer than the other two.) Use four 3-inch nails to secure the center of the X, ensuring that the sharp ends of the nails don't protrude on the far side.
3. Attach the shorter 2x4s to the sides of the X with 3-inch nails, making a solid shape.
4. Repeat with the remaining 2x4s, forming a second X.
5. Use a circular saw to miter the ends of each X so that the Xs have flat, level ends. Doing this will allow the cavalletti to sit flush with the ground. Once you make others, you will also be able to stack the cavalletti to make for a more challenging jump!
6. Stand up the two Xs on level ground, with the longer legs on the ground and the shorter legs at the top. Balance the wooden pole or landscape timber on the Xs. Predrill pilot holes for the lag screws, using the ¼-inch multi-purpose bit. Then, use the recess bit and drill approximately 2 inches into the pole. This will enable the lag screws to fit appropriately, as well as provide the diameter space needed for the 1-inch washers. The washers prevent the head of the lag screw from sinking too deeply into the wood. Drill one hole through the two visible sides of the pole at each X. (Be sure to offset the holes so the screws won't interfere with each other.)
7. Once the holes are complete, use an impact driver or socket wrench to secure the pole to each X using two 4-inch lag screws with 1-inch washers.
8. Apply primer. Let dry and finish using white paint or stain.

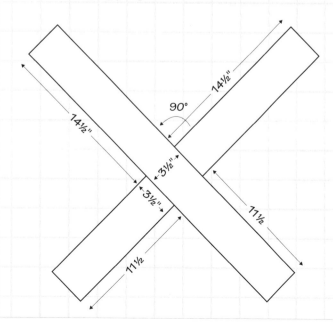

This photo shows the attachment of the X to the pole using lag screws.

Basic Jump Standards

Difficulty Rating: ∩ ∩

Standards purchased from a retailer can range in price from $85 to $200 for a set. If you buy them online, the cost of shipping adds to the expense. We built our set of standards in less than two hours, virtually for free, using materials salvaged from an earlier project. Even if you buy all of the wood, the cost will be less than $50 for a set of standards.

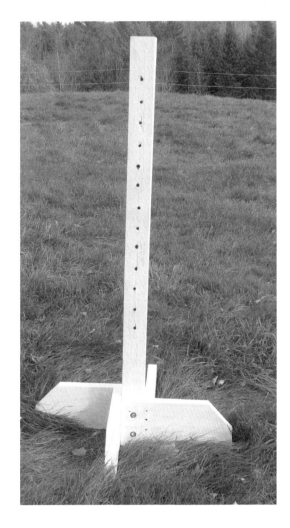

You will want to have several sets of standards to build courses or gymnastic lines. These instructions will help you build one set of 5-foot-tall standards. You can choose to make them 4 feet tall or 6 feet tall instead, depending on how high you are planning to jump. (Note that lumber is sold in 2-foot increments, so to make 5-foot-tall standards you will have to cut off 12 inches from a 6-foot post.)

Standards should be constructed of pressure-treated wood, since they will be exposed to the weather and in contact with the ground almost constantly. Pressure-treated wood is also heavier and will result in a more stable base for your jumps.

Basic Jump Standards

Tools

- Circular saw or miter saw
- Drill or drill press with ⅜-inch bit and ¼-inch multipurpose drill bit
- Screw gun
- Impact driver or socket wrench (if using lag screws)

Materials

- Two 5-foot-long 4x4 posts (pressure-treated)
- Eight 18-inch-long 2x8s (pressure-treated)
- Sixteen 3½-inch lag screws with 1-inch washers, or thirty-two 3½-inch galvanized screws
- Jump cups and pins
- Primer and white outdoor paint

Building the Jump Standards

1. Lay out one of the 4x4 posts: Measure and snap a chalk line down the exact center of the length of one side of the post. (Note that a 4x4 post is actually only 3½ inches wide, so the center will be 1¾ inches from the edge.)

2. Drill holes for the jump cups: Measure and mark a point along the chalk line 18 inches from the bottom. This will be the lowest hole. From this point, measure and mark points along the length of the post every 3 inches, up to the desired height (we drilled holes to accommodate jumps up to 4 feet, 6 inches).

3. Use your ⅜-inch drill bit to drill a hole at each point, straight through the post. Be sure to keep your holes very straight, or it will be difficult to install the jump cups later. If you are

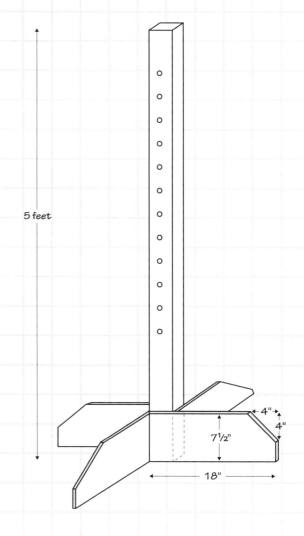

lucky enough to have a drill press, it will make this task much easier and more accurate.

4. Repeat steps 1, 2, and 3 for the second post. Measure and drill carefully to ensure that the holes will line up evenly with those on the first post.

5. Make the supports: First, miter the top outside corners of the eight 2x8 supports. Measure and

Use a drill to bore holes for the jump cups every 3 inches.

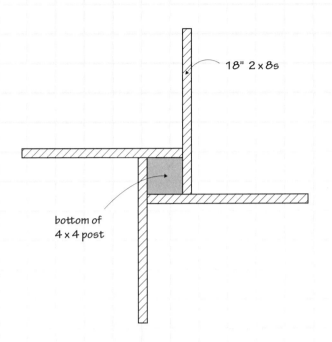

18" 2 x 8s

bottom of
4 x 4 post

mark a point 4 inches from the corner on the top edge, and a point 4 inches from the top corner on the short side (see diagram). Use a miter saw to cut between the two points at a 45-degree angle. If you don't have a miter saw, use a straightedge and a pencil to mark the line, and cut it with a table saw or circular saw. Repeat for the remaining seven supports.

6. Assemble the standards. Use clamps to secure one of the 4x4 posts to a workbench or table-top. Align one of the supports at the bottom of the post, making sure it is level and flush on all sides and along the bottom (see diagram). Predrill 2 pilot holes using a ¼-inch multipur-pose drill bit and use two 3½-inch lag screws and washers to fasten the support to the post. Or, if you do not wish to use such heavy-duty hardware, use four 3½-inch galvanized screws (do not predrill pilot holes).

7. Turn the post a quarter turn and repeat for the second, third, and fourth supports, following the diagram.

Lag Screws

Given that the jump standards will be moved around a riding arena on a regular basis, lag screws will hold the supports to the posts much more securely than screws and can be retightened over time. We highly recommend them. However, they are more expensive to buy and more time-consuming to install. To use a lag screw:

1. First, predrill the hole using a ¼-inch drill bit.
2. Next, drill a recess for the screw head with a 1-inch recess bit.

This drill bit creates a 1-inch recess, into which the head of the lag screw will fit.

3. Insert a 1-inch washer into the recess.
4. Insert the tip of the lag screw and tighten using an impact driver or socket wrench.

Use a socket wrench (shown here) or an impact driver to tighten the lag screws.

Basic Jump Standards cont'd

The arrangement of the feet at the bottom of the standard.

8. Repeat steps 6 and 7 for the second post.

9. Sand, prime, and paint the standards with white paint. Allow appropriate drying time between coats.

10. Install the jump cups using the pins. Jump cups are available from most tack shops and horse supply catalogs. We recommend plastic, rather than metal, cups. If you've ever hit a metal jump cup during a bad fall, you'll know why!

11. Test each hole to make sure the pin slides through easily. If not, carefully use your drill to correct the hole as needed.

Wing Standards

Difficulty Rating: ∩ ∩ ∩

Wing standards are more expensive and time-consuming to construct than basic standards, but they add a classic touch to the jumping arena. If you are planning to have horse shows at your facility, the visual appeal is well worth the effort.

These instructions provide the steps to create one wing of the wing standards. Remember, you will need two wings to complete this project. Simply double the materials below and repeat each step to create two wings.

Wing Standards

Tools

- Drill or drill press with ⅜-inch bit and ¼-inch multipurpose drill bit
- Table saw or circular saw
- Air compressor gun with 3-inch deck nails and 1½-inch finish nails

Materials

- Two 5-foot-tall 4x4 posts (posts)
- Four 24-inch-long 2x6s (feet)
- Two 33-inch-long 1x4s (horizontal pieces)
- Two 39-inch-long 1x3s (vertical)
- Two 42-inch-long 1x3s (vertical)
- One 45-inch-long 1x3 (vertical)

Building the Wing Standards

1. Lay out one of the 4x4 posts. Measure and snap a chalk line down the exact center of the length of one side of the post. (Note that a 4x4 post is actually only 3½ inches wide, so the center will be 1¾ inches from the edge.)

2. Drill holes for the jump cups: Measure and mark a point along the chalk line 18 inches from the bottom. This will be the lowest hole. From this point, measure and mark points along the length of the post every 3 inches, up to the desired height (we drilled holes to accommodate jumps up to 4 feet, 6 inches).

3. Use your ⅜-inch drill bit to drill a hole at each point, straight through the post. Be sure to keep your holes very straight, or it will be difficult to install the jump cups later. If you are lucky enough to have a drill press, it will make this task much easier and more accurate.

4. Repeat steps 1, 2, and 3 for the second post. Measure and drill carefully to ensure that the holes will line up evenly with those on the first post.

5. Make the feet. Cut the top two corners off each of the 2x6s at a 45-degree angle using a miter saw (see photo below).

6. Attach two 2x6s to the bottom of each 4x4 post using 3-inch nails. (Be sure to attach the 2x6s to the solid sides—i.e., without holes—on the post with the jump cup holes.)

7. Using a square, measure and mark a line 6 inches below the tops of the posts. Then, align one 33-inch 1x4 horizontally on both posts as shown in the diagram, ensuring that it is level on the top and plumb on the sides. Use bar clamps to help you align the 1x4. Attach the board using 3-inch decking nails. Test to be

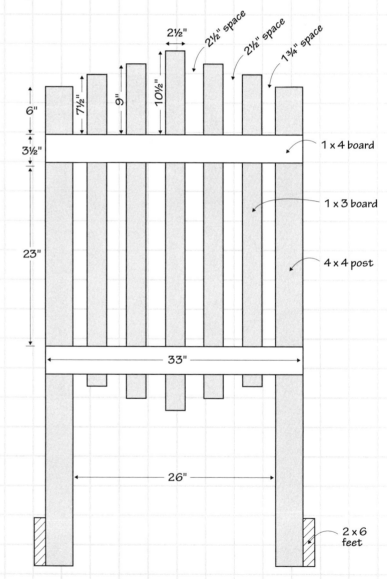

sure the standard will stand up straight on level ground.

8. Mark a line on each of the posts 23 inches below the bottom of the 1x4. Then, align the

This photo shows how the feet are attached to the bottoms of the legs.

second horizontal 1x4 on both posts, following the previous procedure. Attach the board using 3-inch decking nails.

9. Turn the standard over so the 1x4s are face-down. Measure and mark the center points of the horizontal boards (the rails). Attach the 45-inch-long 1x3 (stile) vertically in the center, as shown in the diagram, using 1½-inch finish nails. Allow the board to extend 10½ inches above the top of the top rail.

10. Measure and mark a line on the top and bottom rail 2½ inches out from the sides of the center stile. Align and attach the 42-inch 1x3s along the lines and make sure the tops extend 9 inches above the top of the top rail.

11. Repeat step 2 for the 39-inch 1x3s such that they extend 1½ inches above the top of the top rail.

12. Sand, prime, and paint the standards with white paint. Allow appropriate drying time between coats.

13. Install the jump cups—preferably plastic jump cups—using the pins. Jump cups are available from most tack shops and horse supply catalogs.

14. Test each hole to make sure the pin slides through easily. If not, carefully use your drill to correct the hole as needed.

Option

There are endless patterns to use for wing standards. Try using one 5-foot post and one 4-foot post, and arrange 1x3s in descending order. Instead of using 1x3s, fill in the space with lattice. Make a solid wing using ½-inch plywood as a filler. Flip through the pages of a catalog that sells jumps, and imitate any of the patterns you see.

"Brick" Wall

Difficulty Rating: ∩ ∩ ∩

This simple project can be finished into any of several jump options. It is a basic box, which can be painted to look like a brick or stone wall. Drill holes in the top, and it becomes a flower box. Set it between a pair of wing standards (see page 77) with a jump pole suspended across the top, and it becomes an attractive, very solid-looking jump worthy of any show ring. Made of only a single sheet of ½-inch plywood, this is a very economical project as well.

"Brick" Wall

Tools

- Table saw or circular saw
- Air compressor and finishing nailer
- Screw gun
- Drill with ½-inch bit (for flower box option)
- Random-orbit sander
- 60-and 100-grit sandpaper

Materials

- One 4x8 sheet of ½-inch plywood
- Four 18-inch-long 2x3s
- 1½-inch screws
- 2-inch finish nails

Building the "Brick" Wall

1. Use a table saw or circular saw to cut the plywood into pieces, as shown in the diagram. If you use a circular saw, we recommend that you use a guide, such as a long straightedge clamped to the cutting surface, to help with the accuracy of your cuts.

   The two 7-foot-by-18-inch lengths will be the front and back of the box. The 7-foot-by-11¾-inch strip will be the top of the box. (The bottom will be left open, both to keep the project light and to avoid trapping water inside, which could lead to decay.) The two 11¾-inch-by-18-inch pieces will be the left and right sides of the box. (There will also be a leftover 11¾-inch-by-11¾-inch piece, which is not used in the project.)

2. Align an 18-inch 2x3 to one end of the back 7-foot-by-18-inch piece of plywood. Attach using 1½-inch screws, screwing from the plywood side in. Repeat for the other end of the back piece.

3. Repeat step 2 for the front 7-foot-by-18-inch piece of plywood.

4. Set the 7-foot-by-11¾-inch top piece onto the tops of the front and back pieces, ensuring that the ends and edges of all the pieces are in alignment, and use 2-inch finish nails to secure it.

←— 18" —→	←— 18" —→	←11¾"→
side	side	scrap
front	back	top

11¾"

84"

Accounting for the Kerf: Where Sawdust Comes From

The reason that the top and sides are not a full 12 inches is that when you cut the plywood, the typical blade of a circular or table saw turns ⅛ of an inch of the wood into sawdust with each cut. In woodworking terminology, this is known as the *kerf*. After you make the cuts to form the 18-inch-wide front and back pieces, the width of the remaining plywood for the top will have been reduced by ¼ inch.

"Brick" Wall cont'd

5. Attach the two 18-inch-by-11¾-inch end pieces to the box, screwing them into the 2x3 corner braces with 1½-inch screws.

The 2x3 braces inside the corners of the box hold the plywood sides together.

A horizontal brace lends structural support.

6. Cut three 10¹³⁄₁₆-inch pieces of 2x3 to serve as braces. Turn the box upside down and insert the braces inside the box at equal distances apart, about 6 inches down from the bottom edge of the box. Attach using 1½-inch screws, screwing from the plywood side in.

7. Sand the entire project. Paint the box in a decorative manner to look like a brick wall. Start with a white or off-white base coat for "mortar" over the entire box. Once the base coat is dry, measure and score horizontal lines to help guide you as you paint the "bricks." Then use the broad, flat side of a sponge dipped in brick-red paint like a stamp to apply the brick markings. This is probably the hardest part of the project, for those of us who aren't blessed with artistic skills!

Press the sponge firmly to create mottled rectangles resembling bricks.

8. Finally, following the manufacturer's directions, attach one handle to each end of the box for easier carrying.

Options

For a "stone" wall instead of a brick wall, use a light gray base coat, which will show through between the stones as "mortar," and paint on the stones using two or more darker gray shades. You could even do "brick" on one side and "stone" on the other. Or, paint the box white and then use stencils to spell out the name of your farm or show series.

To make a flower box jump, use a ⅜-inch drill bit to drill holes every six inches along the center of the top. Paint the box white, and insert bouquets of fake flowers into the holes.

Brush Box

Difficulty Rating: ∩ ∩ ∩ ∩

An excellent addition to any arena is a brush box. The box alone can be used as a jump. Stuff the box with brush (real or fake) to increase its height to up to 2 feet. As an option, you can fill the box with potting soil and plant live shrubs or plants in it. (Remember that the weight of the soil and shrubs will make it difficult to move.)

This jump requires a slightly more advanced skill set, but the end result is very elegant. The box is 12 inches high and 3 feet long. An actual jump will need two boxes placed end to end to complete the look. We provide the materials and steps to build just one.

Brush Box

Tools

- Circular saw or miter saw
- Router with both a round-over bit and a ¾-inch straightedge bit
- Air compressor, brad nailer, and finishing nailer
- Jigsaw, handsaw, or wood chisel and mallet
- Screw gun (optional)
- Measuring tape
- Level
- Speed square or framing square
- Two 4-foot pipe clamps

Materials

- Twenty-six 1x4x12-inch pieces of wood (slats for panels)
- Four 2x2x12-inch pieces of wood (corners)
- Four 1x4x34-inch pieces of wood (braces for front and back panels)
- Four 1x4x9½-inch pieces of wood (braces for side panels)
- Two 1x4x13 pieces (trim for left and right sides of top)
- Two 1x4x38 pieces (trim for front and back of top)
- One 10½x35-inch piece of ½-inch CDX-grade plywood (bottom)
- 1¼-inch brad nails or screws
- 2-inch finish nails
- Wood glue

Building the Brush Box

1. Use a router and round-over bit to round off the face edges on the long sides of each piece of the slats and trim pieces. Doing so will give the slats a "tongue-and-groove" look.

2. To make the front panel, lay out two 1x4x34-inch braces parallel to each other, 5 inches apart. Align ten of the 1x4x12-inch slats perpendicular to the 1x4x34-inch boards (as shown in diagram), ensuring that they are square. The slat panel should extend beyond the ends of the perpendicular braces by ½ inch on each side. Secure the 1x4x12s using the brad nailer and 1¼-inch nails.

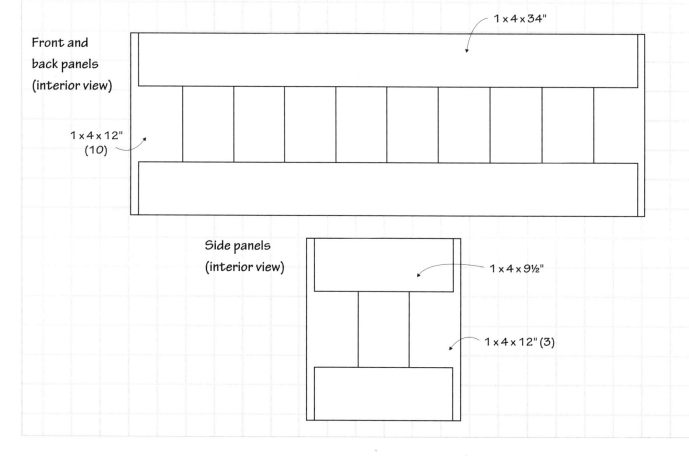

Front and back panels (interior view)

1 x 4 x 34"

1 x 4 x 12" (10)

Side panels (interior view)

1 x 4 x 9½"

1 x 4 x 12" (3)

3. Repeat steps 1 and 2 to make the back panel.

4. To make the side panels, repeat steps 1 and 2, using only three slats per side and the 1x4x9½-inch braces (see diagram).

5. To make grooves on the 2x2x12 corner pieces into which the panels will slide, use a router and ¾-inch straightedge bit. Each corner piece receives two grooves: one for the side panel and one for the front or back panel. Make each groove ⅜-inch deep and ¾-inch wide (see diagram).

6. Now it is time to attach the corners to the four panels. First, apply wood glue to the inside of each of the grooves of one 2x2x12 corner. Then, insert one edge of a side panel into a groove. Make sure you've oriented the grooves so that they will receive their corresponding panels. Now, secure using the finishing nailer and 2-inch finish nails. Repeat this procedure on the other end of the side panel. Then, follow the same procedures to attach the corners to the opposite side panel. Once the corners are attached to the sides, attach the front and back panels into the respective grooves on the corners. You may need to use pipe clamps to help with this assembly process. Last, secure the front and sides to the corners using 2-inch finish nails.

7. To enable the 10½x35-inch plywood bottom to fit, each of its four corners will need to be notched. Make the ⅜x⅜-inch notches using a jigsaw, a handsaw, or a chisel and mallet. Then, insert and attach the plywood bottom using the air compressor, finishing nailer, and 2-inch finish nails.

8. Use a miter saw or circular saw to miter the ends of the four trim boards at 45-degree angles (two at 13 inches long and two at 38 inches long), such that they will frame the top opening of the box, as shown. Attach each piece using 2-inch finish nails. (Note: The trim boards should be positioned so that they create a ½-inch overhang on all sides.)

9. Finish with stain and polyurethane, or paint the box to match your stable colors. Fill the box with an arrangement of brush.

Option

Plant slow-growing shrubs, such as holly or dwarf Alberta spruce trees, in each box. You can keep the spruce trees small by trimming them regularly. To prepare the box for plants, first drill several ¼-inch holes in the plywood bottom to allow drainage, line the bottom with a layer of small stones, and fill the box with potting soil. (Note: Once filled with soil, the box will be quite heavy, so be sure to position it first before adding the soil and shrubs.)

Picket Gate

Difficulty Rating: ∩ ∩ ∩

The surprisingly easy-to-build picket gate is a classic show jump, which can be hung from the jump standards at any height. This gate is 24 inches high, but you can make it smaller (12 inches) or larger (up to 3 feet). Typically painted white, the gate can also be painted in your stable colors. Combine it with jump poles and basic jump standards (page 73) to make an airy yet visible jump.

Picket Gate

Tools

- Table saw or miter saw
- Air compressor gun with 1½-inch finish nails, or screw gun and 1⅝-inch screws
- Framing square

Materials

- One 10-foot-long 2x4 board (top rail)
- One 8-foot-long 2x4 board (bottom rail)
- Eighteen 1x4x24-inch boards (slats)

Building the Picket Gate

1. Lay out the 10-foot 2x4 and the 8-foot 2x4, parallel and 24 inches apart. Measure and mark a line 12 inches from each end of the 10-foot rail.
2. Align one 1x4x24 slat at each end of the 8-foot rail, lining it up with the mark on the 10-foot rail, as shown. Use a framing square to ensure that each end is square. Attach these two slats using the nail gun or screw gun.
3. Arrange the eighteen 1x4x24 slats as shown, 2¼ inches apart. Attach the slats to the 2x4s using the nail gun or screws. If you happen to have a table saw, it is helpful to make a spacer jig out of scrap wood that is exactly 2¼ inches wide, and use it to mark the gap between each slat from the previous one. Doing so helps with spacing accuracy and saves a lot of time measuring for and marking spaces. Simply use the spacer to align the next slat, attach the slat with nails or screws, and move on to the next slat following the same method.
4. Sand, paint, or stain the picket gate.

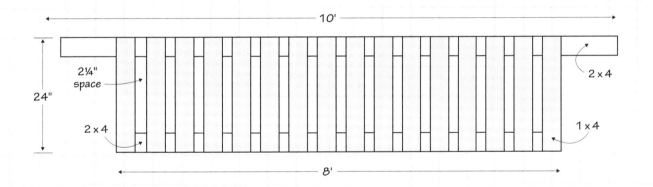

CHAPTER 6

Horse Clothing

Just as the chapters on wood projects presume at least a little knowledge of woodworking, this chapter assumes that the reader knows at least a little bit about how to sew. If not, books are available that teach basic sewing skills.

Some general notes:

- Familiarize yourself with your sewing machine before you begin a project. Every sewing machine is slightly different, so be sure you know how to wind a bobbin and thread the machine. Run some test stitches on scrap material to practice and get a feel for the machine.
- When beginning or ending a seam, sew three or four stitches, then stop and backstitch (run the machine in reverse) over the first few stitches. Then continue on with the seam. This locks the threads to prevent the seam from unraveling.
- To stitch around a corner, stop the machine while the needle is deep into the fabric. (Use the hand-crank to position the needle exactly where you want the corner to be.) Lift the presser foot and turn the fabric so it is oriented in the new direction. Lower the presser foot and continue stitching.
- Many of the materials used in these projects are fairly thick—Velcro, fleece, and quilted cotton. For best results and durability, use a heavy-duty needle and thread.

Polo Wraps

Difficulty Rating: ∩

Polo wraps are easy to make, and can be customized to fit your horse. They are used to protect the delicate tendons of the horse's lower legs during jumping or other strenuous work. The traditional color for dressage horses is white, but since polos are used only for schooling, never at shows, it can be fun to use bright colors or crazy patterns instead (leopard print, anyone?). If you aren't sure how to apply a polo wrap correctly, ask a trainer or other knowledgeable person to show you how. Incorrectly wrapped polos can cause injury.

If you choose to add an appliqué to the ends of the wraps, it's best to choose one that looks the same whether it is right side up or upside down. If you choose an image with a "top," such as the butterflies on my polos below, you'll need to be careful to make a left-side wrap and a right-side wrap, and mark the far ends so that when the wraps are rolled up, you'll be able to tell which is which. If you put the right-side wrap on the left leg, or vice versa, the decoration will be upside down.

Polo Wraps

Tools

- Sewing machine
- Scissors
- Rotary cutter and mat
- Chalk line
- Pins

Materials

- 3 yards of synthetic fleece
- Four 7-inch-long 1½-inch-wide hook-and-loop closures
- Thread

Making the Polo Wraps

1. If the fleece has a hem or edging, trim it off before you begin. Cut four strips of fleece, each 3 yards long and 4½ inches wide. (For a pony, use 2½ yards long by 3 inches wide.) An easy way to create a straight line to cut along is to use a carpenter's chalk line. Measure 4½ inches in at each end of the fleece, and snap a chalk line between the two points. (The chalk can easily be brushed or washed off later.) You can use scissors to carefully cut along the line, but a rotary cutter (available at craft and fabric stores) will cut faster and straighter.

2. Lay out one strip of fleece cut to length and width. At one end of the strip, fold down each corner to form a triangle. Pin in place.

3. Align one strip of the hook (hard) side of the hook-and-loop material, business side up, so that its bottom edge meets the bottom of the folded triangle. Pin in place (see photo).

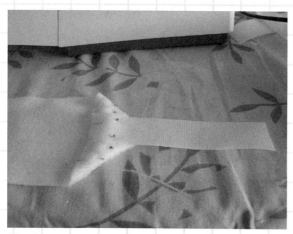

Pin the wrap into a triangle, and pin the Velcro strip in place.

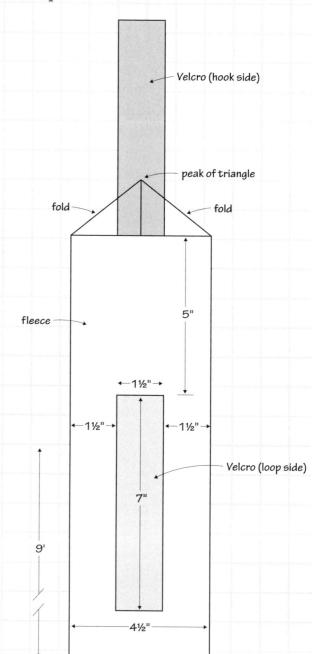

Fleece is sold in 60-inch widths, so one piece of fleece will provide enough material for thirteen polo wraps! This comes in handy if you make a few mistakes in the learning process. You can also use the leftover material for another project.

4. Sew straight across the bottom of the triangle. Sew a second seam in the shape of a "house," as shown.

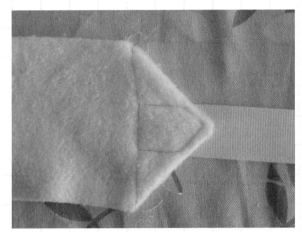

The "house"-shaped stitch pattern. I used light blue thread to make the pattern more visible for the photo, but you should match the thread color to the fabric color.

5. Turn the strip of fleece over. Measure 5 inches in from the bottom of the triangle. Center the corresponding (soft) strip of hook-and-loop material on the fleece. Pin in place.

6. Sew around the edge of the hook-and-loop strip.
7. Remove all pins.
8. Repeat steps 1 through 7 for each of the remaining three wraps.

Option

If desired, decorate the wraps using iron-on patches, glitter glue, or sewn-on decorations. (Note: If using iron-on patches, remember that a hot iron can shrink the fleece material. Keep the iron on a low setting without steam, and cover the fleece with a piece of thin cloth to protect it further.) We used iron-on butterfly patches, sewn on for added durability. When adding embellishments, always keep in mind the horse's safety, and do not use anything with sharp or rough edges. Always apply on the outside of the ends of the wraps, never where they may come in contact with the horse's skin.

Locate the patch halfway between the soft Velcro and the end of the point.

Memory-Foam Saddle Pad

Difficulty Rating: ∩ ∩ ∩

Memory foam is a high-density, shock-absorbing material made famous by its use in Tempur-Pedic® mattresses. It is now possible to purchase thin sheets of memory foam, sold as "mattress toppers," relatively inexpensively. This material makes a great cushion under a saddle. These instructions make a memory-foam pad with a washable cover. After use, remove the memory-foam insert to machine-wash the cover as needed. We made a white cover for a classic look, but a colored cover could be made to match your polo wraps or other gear.

These instructions were inspired by our friend Anne Ward, a student at Cornell vet school, who was looking for a solution for her sore-backed mare.

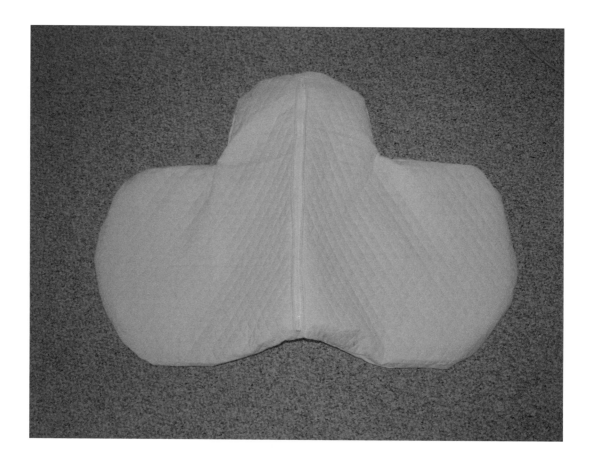

Memory-Foam Saddle Pad

Tools

- Sewing machine with heavy-gauge needle
- Scissors or rotary cutter and mat

Materials

- 1-inch-thick memory-foam mattress topper, available online or at home goods stores
- 2 yards quilted material or fleece
- Heavy-duty thread
- 1½-inch-wide zipper (20 inches long)

Making the Memory-Foam Saddle Pad

1. Determine the size needed. This will vary depending on your saddle. Find an existing saddle pad that fits your saddle well. (For a Western saddle, use a square pad. For an English saddle, use a shaped pad.) Measure the length of the pad from pommel to cantle. Measure the width of the pad from flap to flap. These are the measurements needed for the memory-foam insert. So, if your existing pad is 18 inches long by 24 inches wide, cut the insert to 18 x 24. You can use the actual pad as a template, tracing around it onto the foam and then cutting just inside that line.

2. Add 4 inches to each measurement to determine the amount of material needed for the top and bottom cover. (So for the example above, the covers are 22 x 28.) It is easiest to trace the existing saddle pad onto the "wrong" side of the material with chalk or marking pen, and then cut around the line, leaving a 2-inch margin around the edges. Cut through two layers of fabric at once to produce both the top and bottom covers at the same time.

3. Cut a 20-inch slit straight down the spine of the top cover. This will allow for the zipper to be added. Fold over a ¼-inch hem along each

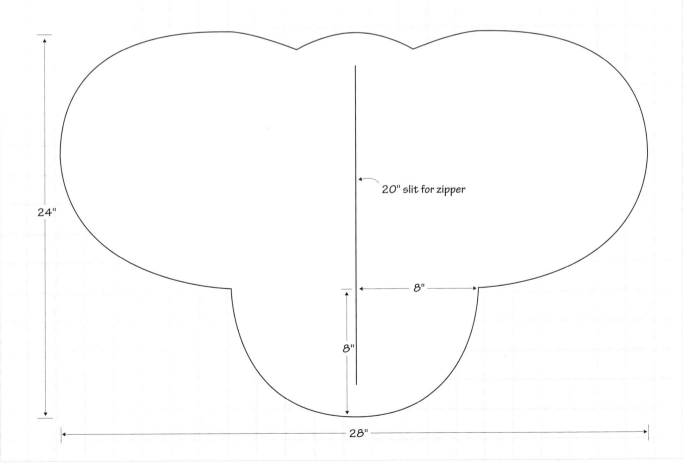

Memory-Foam Saddle Pad cont'd

side of the slit; then, pin and sew. Remove pins.

4. Pin the zipper to the underside of the hemmed edges of the top cover. Sew and remove pins.

5. Sew the top and bottom together. Lay out the bottom cover with the underside facing down ("good" side up). Align the top cover on the bottom cover with its underside facing up ("good" side facing the bottom cover). Pin in place.

6. Sew the top cover to the bottom cover all the way around the perimeter, 1 inch in from the edge of the material.

7. Unzip the zipper and turn the cover right side out.

8. Insert the memory foam into the cover and zip the zipper.

Quarter Sheet

Difficulty Rating: ∩ ∩ ∩

A quarter sheet is an important piece of horse clothing for cold climates, designed for riding a clipped or thin-coated horse in freezing temperatures. The sheet fits behind the saddle, over the horse's hindquarters (hence the name), to keep his back and hips warm. These instructions will help you make a quarter sheet that can be used either under the saddle flaps or over the rider's legs, helping you to stay warm as well. The Velcro closure allows the rider to easily remove the quarter sheet after warming up, and to put it back on for the cool-down part of the ride. Making your own sheet allows you to customize the weight and color of the sheet. Add ribbons, patches, or monogramming for a personalized look.

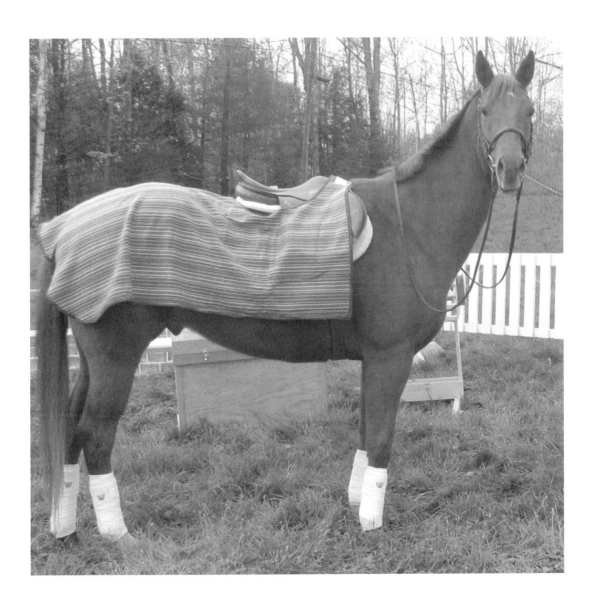

Quarter Sheet

Tools

- Scissors
- Rotary cutter and mat
- Chalk line
- Chalk or marking pen
- Sewing machine
- Pins

Materials

- 2 yards of 60-inch-wide fleece material
- 9 yards of extra-wide double-fold fleece binding or other trim material
- 2-inch-wide-by-6-inch-long hook-and-loop closure
- 24-inch length of braided cord, the same color as the ribbon

Making the Quarter Sheet

1. First, determine the size sheet needed. Measure the length of your horse from just behind his elbow, where the girth goes, to the back of his hindquarters (A). Measure the distance from one stifle up over the hindquarters to the other stifle (B) (see diagram). Measurement A is the overall length of the piece of fabric. Measurement B is the overall width of the fabric.

2. Measure and cut a large rectangle of fleece that is A long by B wide. (In my case, this

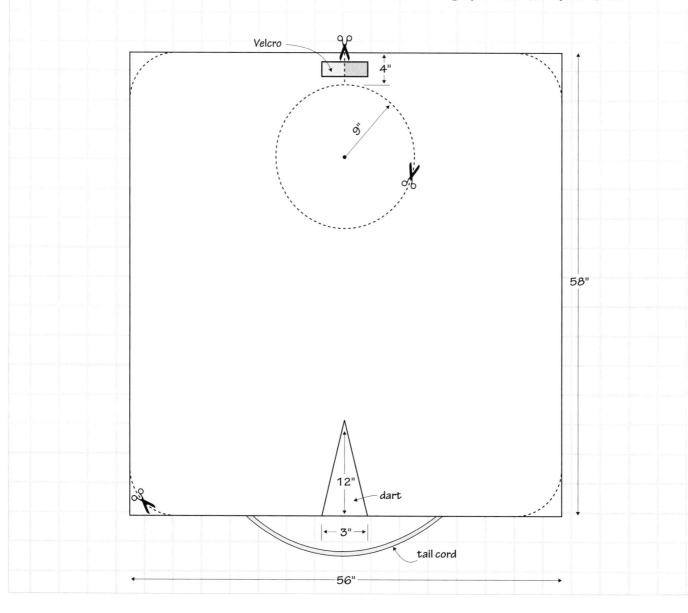

was 58 inches by 56 inches.) Cutting a long, straight line is easiest to accomplish by using a rotary cutter. Make a line to follow using a carpenter's chalk line. If the fleece came with a finished edge, trim it off.

3. Following the diagram, draw an 18-inch-diameter circle of fabric at the front center of the fleece rectangle, leaving 4 inches of fabric at the front. To draw the circle, measure a center point 13 inches from the front edge of the fabric. Set a measuring tape to 9 inches, and measure and mark multiple points around the circumference of a circle, 9 inches from the center point. Cut a slit through the center of the 4-inch strip as shown on the template, and then cut out the circle that you drew.

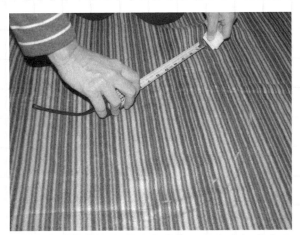

Use a measuring tape or ruler and chalk to mark out the 18-inch-diameter circle.

4. Cut and sew a dart at the center of the back of the sheet, following the instructions below.
5. Pin the fleece binding along the entire edge of the fleece so it covers the raw edge. Sew using a sewing machine, and remove the pins.
6. Pin the Velcro closure to the slit in the front of the sheet, following the diagram. Pin the hook piece to one side of the slit, and the loop piece to the other side of the slit, so the two pieces will hold the sheet closed over the top of the horse's withers. Sew the Velcro onto the sheet using a sewing machine, and remove the pins.
7. Pin and sew the 24-inch cord to the center back of the sheet. (At the fabric store we found a curtain tieback that worked perfectly for this!)

This will be a tail cord to pass under the horse's tail, holding the sheet down when in use. Remove the pins, and double-check the entire sheet to be sure all pins have been removed.

Option

Add iron-on patches, or use your sewing machine's monogramming option (if available) to personalize your sheet.

How to Sew a Dart

1. **Mark dart, following the shape on the diagram below. The center line should be 12 inches long. Mark the point of the dart with a horizontal line.**
2. **Fold dart on center line, matching stitching lines and markings at the wide end, the point, and in between. Pin in place, with heads of pins facing toward the folded edge for easy removal as you stitch.**
3. **Stitch along the line, from the wide end to the point of the dart.**
4. **Open and "squash" down the flap of fabric so it lies flat, and stitch it down to the underlying fabric.**

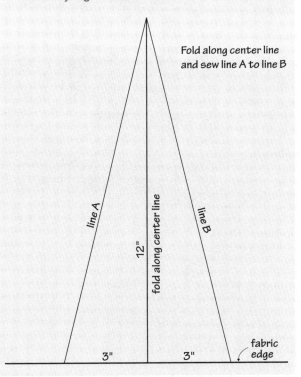

Fold along center line and sew line A to line B

line A

line B

12"
fold along center line

3"   3"   fabric edge

Fleece Cooler

Difficulty Rating: ∩ ∩ ∩

This sheet can serve as a dress sheet, cooler, or blanket liner. A dress sheet is used at a show to cover the horse between classes, keeping off chilly air and making him look fancy. A cooler is used after a ride when the horse is sweaty. The wicking fabric draws moisture away from his body, while keeping his muscles warm and allowing them to cool down slowly. A blanket liner is used under a turnout sheet or blanket for an extra layer of warmth. The instructions describe a sheet made of fleece, but you could also make a wool cooler by using a wool blanket as a source of fabric.

Fleece Cooler

Tools

- Scissors
- Rotary cutter and mat
- Sewing machine
- Pins

Materials

- 3 yards of 60-inch-wide fleece material
- 9 yards of extra-wide double-fold fleece binding or other trim material
- 2-inch-wide-by-6-inch-long Velcro closure
- 8-inch-by-8-inch square of thick white fleece
- 24-inch length of braided cord, the same color as the ribbon

Making the Fleece Sheet

1. First, determine the size sheet needed. Measure the length of your horse from the front center of his chest to the back point of his hindquarters. (In my case, this was 78 inches.)

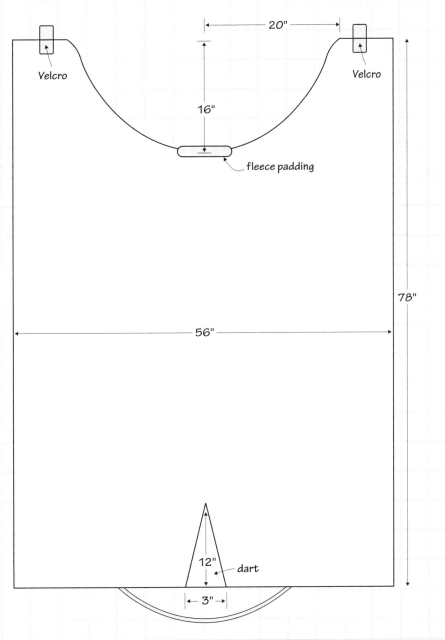

Fleece Cooler cont'd

This is the overall length of the piece of fabric. To make the sheet as wide as possible, use the entire width of the piece of fleece. Measure and cut the fleece to length using a rotary cutter. Make a line to follow using a carpenter's chalk line. If the fleece came with a finished edge, trim it off.

2. As shown in the photo below, fold the fleece rectangle in half lengthwise and, cutting through both layers of fabric, cut out the corner from the folded side. Make the cut 16 inches back and 20 inches down from the front top corner (see diagram). This cutout will allow for the horse's neck when the sheet is in use.

Fold the fabric in half and use a rotary cutter to cut through both layers at once, ensuring symmetry.

3. Cut and sew a dart at the center of the back of the sheet. (See sidebar under Quarter Sheet on page 97.)
4. Pin the fleece binding along the entire edge of the fleece so it covers the raw edge. Sew using a sewing machine, and remove the pins.
5. Pin the Velcro closure to the chest opening of the sheet, as shown. Pin the hook piece to one side of the chest, and the loop piece to the other side of the chest, so the two pieces will hold the sheet closed in front of the horse's chest. Sew the Velcro onto the sheet using a sewing machine, and remove the pins.
6. Cut an 8-inch-by-8-inch square of thick, white fleece. Fold each of two sides in toward the

middle so they meet in the center, and stitch them down. (Don't forget to change the color of the thread on your machine to white!) Locate the center of the front of the sheet, where the horse's withers will be, and fold the square over the hem at that point. Stitch it in place.

7. Pin and sew the 24-inch cord to the center back of the sheet. This will be a tail cord to pass under the horse's tail, holding the sheet down when in use. Remove the pins, and double-check the entire sheet to be sure all pins have been removed.

Option

Add iron-on patches, or use your sewing machine's monogramming option (if available) to personalize your sheet.

Width of the Sheet and Horse Size

Fleece fabric is sold in 60-inch widths. For an average 15- to 16-hand horse, this is about the right width to make a well-fitting sheet. (The horse in the photo is 16 hands.) For a very small horse or pony, you may choose to make the sheet narrower (so it won't hang down as far on the pony's sides). Measure the horse from one elbow, up over the withers, to the other elbow, and cut the fabric to this width.

For a very large or wide horse, 60 inches will not be wide enough. In this case, you'll have to use two pieces of fleece sewn together along the spine. It's not ideal, since if the seam is not perfect it will be fairly visible, but if you have a big horse, that is what you will have to do.

Another option for large horses is to find or buy a queen- or king-size fleece or wool blanket, and use it as material for the sheet. Dimensions vary, but a queen-size blanket will allow you to make a sheet that is as much as 76 inches wide, and a king is even larger.

Saddle Cover

Difficulty Rating: ∩ ∩

You can use almost any lightweight material for the saddle cover, but we like to use fleece since it is slightly stretchy and soft enough that you won't risk marring the saddle. The project is quick and easy to sew. It does require a bit of artistic ability when marking out and cutting the fabric, but the elasticity of the edging will cover a multitude of small errors. If you're unsure, err on the side of too big rather than too small.

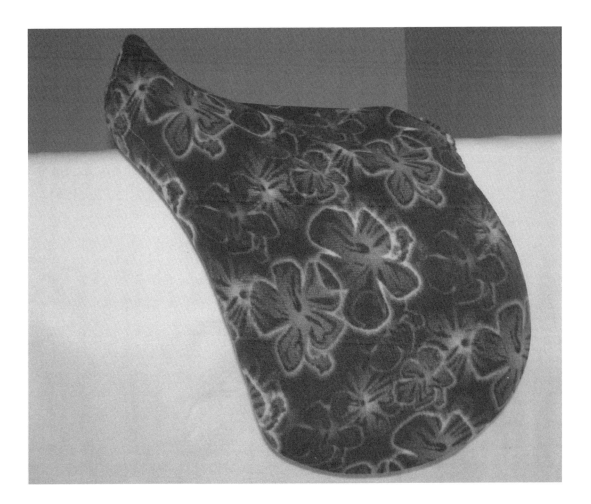

Saddle Cover

Tools

- Sewing machine
- Scissors
- Pins

Materials

- 1½ yards of material (fleece, linen, or an old sheet or blanket)
- 3 yards of ½-inch-wide elastic
- Thread

Making the Saddle Cover

1. Transfer the shape of the template below to the material. Cut out the shape using scissors. (The template will work for a typical 16- to 18-inch close contact or all-purpose English saddle. Add an extra 2 inches all around for a larger saddle, or remove 2 inches for a child or pony saddle. For a dressage saddle, increase the length of the flaps by 2 inches each.)

2. With the underside of the material facing up, fold the edge of the material over, creating a 1-inch-deep hem, and pin it in place. This hem will form a tube for the elastic to slide into. Before sewing, carefully lay the cover over your saddle to be sure it fits accurately. The hem should be at least 2 inches larger than the saddle all the way around. Make adjustments as needed.

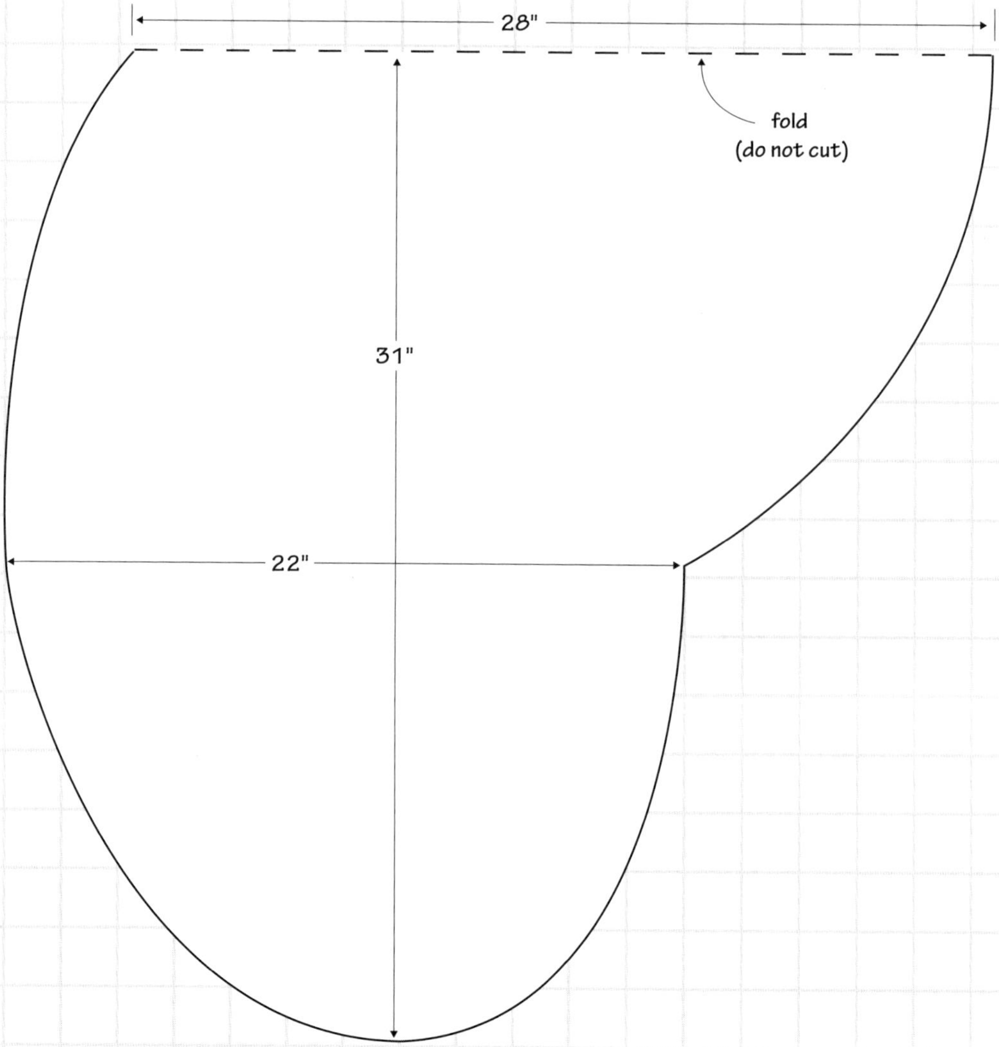

28"

fold
(do not cut)

31"

22"

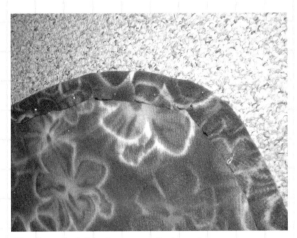

The hem is folded over and pinned to create a 1-inch tube.

3. Stitch the entire hem using a sewing machine. Start and end the seam at the cantle, and leave a 1-inch opening at the end of the seam. Remove all pins.

4. Slide the elastic into the hem through the 1-inch opening. This step is tedious and time-consuming, so be patient!

5. When the elastic is all the way through the hem, pin the ends together loosely at the opening in the hem. Place the saddle cover onto your saddle and pull the elastic tight, so that the hem scrunches together on the underside of the saddle. When you are happy with the way the saddle cover fits, knot the elastic together at that point and remove the cover from the saddle.

6. Cut the elastic to the appropriate length, as marked by the knot. Overlap the ends of the elastic by 1 inch and sew them together with several rows of stitches, by hand or machine.

7. Sew shut the 1-inch opening in the hem.

Option

Add monogramming, embroidery, or patches to the saddle cover.

CHAPTER 7

Projects for a Rainy Day

This chapter has a few projects that are easy for kids and parents to do together, or for campers to do during craft hour. They take very little time to make, and the results are rewarding for children.

The most difficult project in this chapter is the Memorial Frame. This project is best for adults, or older children with adult supervision, and it does require the use of a router or table saw.

Appliquéd Jeans

Difficulty Rating: ∩

This project is very easy to make, and takes very little time. It's a great choice for a camp project or a snow day when kids are home from school. Sewing skills are not needed—just a little creativity! The fusible web is a plastic material that melts under the heat of an iron, fusing two separate pieces of fabric together. One common brand is Steam-A-Seam, but others are also available online or in any sewing supply or fabric store.

If you're making this project with a group of children, provide a variety of different-patterned fabrics and let each kid choose her own motif. Each child should also bring an article of clothing. Kids will have lots of fun creating their own unique items and showing them off to each other.

Appliquéd Jeans

Tools

- Scissors
- Iron
- Needle and thread, sewing machine, or colored craft glue

Materials

- Item of clothing, such as a pair of jeans or a fleece or denim jacket
- Fusible web fabric such as Steam-A-Seam (see Resources)
- Scrap of horse-themed print fabric

Making the Appliquéd Jeans

1. Select an item of clothing, such as an old pair of jeans.
2. Choose a particular horse motif from the horse-print fabric. Pin it to a piece of fusible web, with the "wrong" side facing the web. (Note: It is easiest if you choose an image that has smooth, regular edges rather than jagged, irregular ones.)
3. Carefully cut around the outline of the horse motif with scissors, cutting through both the fabric and the fusible web simultaneously. Remove the pins.
4. Align the fabric and fusible web on the garment in the desired location. For jeans, you can cover a hole in the knee, or put the patch on the back pocket or outside of the lower leg. For a jacket, pin the patch to the left front chest or in the center of the back.
5. Iron the patch onto the garment. The fusible web will melt, fusing the patch to the fabric.
6. Using a sewing machine or a needle and embroidery thread in a contrasting color, sew a bulky seam around the edge of the patch to frame it visually, as well as to make the patch more durable. An easier option is to carefully frame the patch with a single line of colored craft glue.

Option

You can use this method on almost any item of clothing—horse or human! Try it on a saddle pad, sheet, sweatshirt, T-shirt, handbag, duffel bag, or backpack.

Align the fabric cutout over the fusible web on the item of clothing before ironing it in place.

Chewy Carrot-Apple Treats

Difficulty Rating: Ω]

Horses love treats! These treats are easy and fun to make, with all of a horse's favorite flavors, including apples, carrots, oats, and molasses. They are healthy and delicious for horses. They're edible for humans as well, but personally we find them a bit too salty for our taste.

Try this project on a snowy or rainy day. This is a fun one for children, pony clubbers, or campers as well. You can customize these treats by adding your horse's favorite flavors, or by forming the cookies into fun shapes.

Chewy Carrot-Apple Treats

Tools

- Large mixing bowl
- Grater or food processor
- Spoon
- Measuring cup
- Cookie sheet
- Oven

Materials

- 2 cups rolled oats or oatmeal
- 2 carrots
- 1 large apple
- ¾ cup dark molasses
- ⅓ cup vegetable oil
- 1 Tbsp salt
- ¾ cup flour

Making the Treats

1. Grate the carrots and apple using a hand grater or a food processor.

Assemble your ingredients.

2. Mix all the ingredients in a large bowl. Batter will be very sticky. If it is too wet to handle, refrigerate it for an hour to firm it up.
3. Drop the mixture by small, bite-size teaspoonfuls onto the cookie sheet.
4. Bake for 20 minutes in a 350-degree oven.
5. Transfer treats to a cooling rack and allow to cool completely before feeding.

Option

Add other ingredients depending on your horse's taste; for example, ½ cup mashed banana, ¼ cup raisins, ½ cup ground flax (for omega-3s!), or a few drops of peppermint oil.

Horseshoe Picture Frame

Difficulty Rating: ∩

This very simple project is quick to make on a rainy afternoon or at camp. It puts to use the old horseshoes lying around the barn.

Horseshoe Picture Frame

Tools

- Hammer
- Scissors
- Hole punch or awl

Materials

- Horseshoe
- Paint
- Photograph of your horse
- Cardboard or foam-core board
- Clear, lightweight plastic sheet (such as a "document protector," in the office supply aisle)
- Raffia, ribbon, or string
- Superglue

Making the Horseshoe Picture Frame

1. If the horseshoe has toe clips, clamp it down on a sturdy work surface and pound the clips with a hammer so that they bend over. The clips will help to hold the photo in place later on.

Clamp the horseshoe to a solid work surface before pounding down the toe clips.

2. Clean the horseshoe well, removing any dirt and using a wire brush to scrub off as much rust as possible.

3. Paint the horseshoe black, or any other color, with acrylic craft paint, and allow it to dry overnight.

4. Using the horseshoe as a template, trace its shape onto a piece of cardboard or foam-core board. Mark straight across the top (open) part of the shoe.

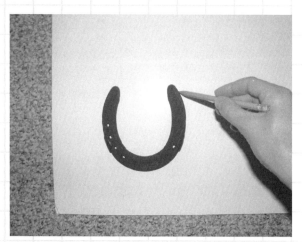

Trace around the outside of the horseshoe with a pencil.

5. Cut out the cardboard shape, just inside the line you traced. Hold the cutout against the back of the horseshoe and check to see if any of it shows around the edges. Trim as needed for a perfect fit. If the shoe has toe clips, use them to support the cardboard.

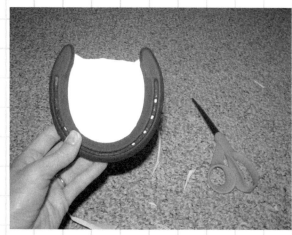

Check to be sure none of the cardboard shows around the edges, and trim as necessary.

6. Using the cardboard as a template, cut the photograph of your horse and the clear plastic into the same shape. Before cutting, hold the shoe against the photo to make sure it lines up nicely, without cutting off any important parts of the photo. Not every photo will work. Photos with a vertical orientation are most likely to fit well into the frame.

7. Align the plastic sheet and the photograph on the back of the horseshoe so that the photo shows through the front, with the plastic covering the image. Fit the cardboard onto the back. Push a needle or awl through the nail holes on the horseshoe, piercing through the plastic, photo, and cardboard backing. Or, use a pen to mark the locations of the nail holes, and then remove the materials from the shoe and use a hole punch to make holes.

8. Replace the plastic, photo, and cardboard into the shoe and line up the holes. Weave the raffia, ribbon, or string through the holes on the horseshoe so that they "sew" the photo and backing materials into place. The two ends should come out through the top two holes at the front. (If they come out the back, the photo will not hang properly.) Tie the ends into an attractive bow. Hang the horseshoe picture frame from a nail or hook using the string.

Option

Buy a brass nameplate engraved with your horse's name and attach it across the top of the horseshoe using hot glue or superglue.

Memorial Frame

Difficulty Rating: ∩ ∩ ∩

This picture frame is a beautiful and classy way to remember the equine friends who are no longer with us. The upper part of the frame allows space for a horizontal 5x7 photo in a mat, or an 8x10 photo without a mat. The lower part of the frame houses a horseshoe, or another photo. The center cross-piece is a good place to put a nameplate or plaque. Use the nameplate from your horse's actual halter (if you have one), or you can order a custom plate from your local tack shop or equestrian catalog.

The frame can also be used to remember a particular event. Mount a photo from the event, attach a plaque describing name and date of the event, and in the lower space, hang a ribbon or medal won at that event.

Memorial Frame

Tools

- Router
- Miter saw or miter box and handsaw
- Wood glue
- 1¼-inch brad nails (18-gauge)
- Brad nailer
- Crown stapler
- ¾-inch crown staples
- Framing clamps
- Random-orbit sander
- 100-grit and 220-grit sandpaper
- Stain or polyurethane

Materials

- One 6-foot piece of furniture-grade 1x2 poplar, maple, or other hardwood
- An 8x10 sheet of framing glass
- A photograph of your horse
- A mat for a 5x7 photo (outside measurements will be 8x10)
- Solid piece of 8x10 matting that matches the 5x7 photo mat
- Two pieces of 8x10 cardboard
- Horseshoe
- Florist's wire or fishing line
- Framing hardware

Making the Memorial Frame

1. Use a ½-inch straight bit on a router mounted to a router table to make a ½-inch-wide-by-¼-inch deep rabbet cut along one edge of the 1x2.

2. Cut the 1x2s to the lengths shown, using a compound miter saw or a miter box and handsaw, with 45-degree miter cuts. The shorter sides should be the side with the rabbet cut. Two pieces need to measure 12 inches at the longest point and two pieces need to measure 18⅜ inches at the longest point. Keep the leftover wood, which will be used to make the cross-piece in step 4.

3. Assemble the four sides into a frame clamp. We recommend using a Stanley's 90-degree corner clamp, which is an inexpensive route (especially if you buy only one) or a threaded rod frame. In any case, adjust the framing clamp until each corner aligns in an accurate

45-degree angle. When ready, glue the ends of the boards, join, and tighten the clamp(s). Once the glue has dried, remove clamps and reinforce the joints using 1¼-inch brad nails.

4. To make the cross-piece, cut the remaining piece of 1x2 from step 1 to length (10 inches). Then, rabbet-cut the other edge of the board, using the same router setup from step 1. Next,

The cross-piece resembles a long T-shape.

Use corner clamps to press the joint together while the wood glue dries.

Memorial Frame cont'd

set the blade of a table saw or router to a height of ¼ inch. Flip the cross-piece over, and cut ½ inch off the top side of the board on each end (the top side is the opposite side of the rabbet cuts), forming an elongated T-shape.

5. Add the cross-piece: The cross-piece creates the top and bottom framing spaces. Measure 8 inches down from the inside of the top rabbet cut on both sides of the 1x2 main frame and mark with a pencil. Align the cross-piece so that the inside of the rabbet cut on the cross-piece aligns with the mark. Each space should now measure 8 inches by 10 inches. Glue the ends of the cross-piece and clamp using a bar clamp. When the glue has dried, remove the clamp and reinforce the joints using ¾-inch crown staples.

6. Sand the frame lightly with 100-grit sandpaper, removing all visible wood glue. Finish the frame as desired with stain, clear finish, or paint. Allow to dry.

7. Turn the frame over and insert glass into the upper 8x10 space. Insert photo mat. Insert photo and tape in place.

8. Mount the horseshoe to the solid mat using wire or fishing line pushed through the mat and twisted in back.

9. Insert the horseshoe and mat into the lower frame space.

10. Place 8x10 pieces of cardboard in the top and bottom of the back of the frame.

11. Use frame hardware to secure the cardboard backing to the frame, and to prepare the frame for hanging.

Insert the cross-piece into the frame and glue it in place.

Resources

Horse Information and Books

www.101horsekeepingtips.com

www.horsecity.com

www.lyonspress.com

www.westernhorseman.com

Wood and Woodworking Supplies

www.homedepot.com

www.lowes.com

www.rockler.com

Fabric and Sewing Supplies

www.fabric.com

www.fabricdepot.com

www.joann.com

www.milldirecttextiles.com

www.overstock.com

www.wholesaleapplique.com

Index

Note

Give a man a fish and you feed him for a day. Teach him how to fish and you feed him for a lifetime.

—Lao Tzu

We enjoyed inventing and creating the projects in this book, and we hope you will enjoy making them. But more important, we hope that the skills and techniques you learn will enable you to develop and build or sew your own project ideas around the farm. We've included several pages at the back of the book to encourage you to explore your own concepts. Use them to note measurements, jot down ideas, and draw schematic diagrams. Have fun!

Notes and Rough Sketches

Notes and Rough Sketches

Notes and Rough Sketches

Notes and Rough Sketches

About the Authors

Jessie and Jason Shiers live in Norway, Maine, with their daughter and their horses. Their work has been published in *Western Horseman* magazine. Jessie is the author of several horse books including *Knack Grooming Horses* and *101 Horsekeeping Tips,* and is the co-author of *The Lyons Press Horseman's Dictionary.*

Training, Riding, and Caring for Your Horse

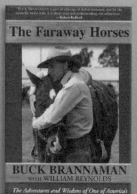
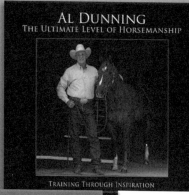
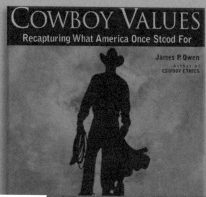

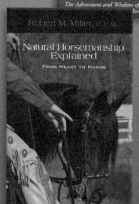

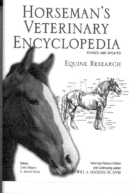

⭐ Natural horsemanship

⭐ Western and English training

⭐ Horse care and health

⭐ Dressage

⭐ Literature for horse enthusiasts

For a complete listing of all our titles, please visit our Web site at www.LyonsPress.com.